D1121688

DATE DUE

Dec 97			

FIRST LIGHT

FIRST LIGHT
Modern Bahrain and its Heritage

HAMAD BIN ISA AL KHALIFA

KEGAN PAUL INTERNATIONAL
London and New York

hed in English in 1994 by
Kegan Paul International Limited
UK: P.O. Box 256, London WC1B 3SW, England
USA: 562 West 113th Street, New York, NY 10025, USA

Distributed by
John Wiley & Sons Limited
Southern Cross Trading Estate
1 Oldlands Way, Bognor Regis
West Sussex, PO22 9SA, England

Columbia University Press
562 West 113th Street
New York, NY 10025, USA

© Hamad bin Isa Al Khalifa 1994

Phototypeset in 10/12pt Palatino
by Intype, London

Printed in Great Britain by TJ Press, Padstow, Cornwall

ISBN 0 7103 0494 3

British Library Cataloguing in Publication Data
Al Khalifa, Hamad Bin Isa
    First Light: Modern Bahrain and Its
    Heritage
    I. Title
    953.65

ISBN 0–7103–0494–3

US Library of Congress Cataloging in Publication Data
Āl Khalīfah, Hamad Ibn Īsá.
    First light : modern Bahrain and its heritage / Hamad bin Isa Al
Khalifa.
        152 pp.   20 cm.
    ISBN 0–7103–0494–3 : $50.00 (U.S.)
        1. Bahrain—History.   I. Title.
DS247.B25A65   1994
953.65—dc20   94–10622
                                                                CIP

Contents

In the name of God,
the Merciful, the Compassionate

Preface

We who have grown up and lived under the skies of Bahrain owe our nation a weighty obligation. The love we hold for our homeland is in the spirit of our religion which confirms that patriotism is an article of faith. Just as there are patriots in the history of every people who sacrificed to serve the nation which nurtured and protected them, our tradition tells of the many who have shed their blood for this land and given everything for its sake. God grant that we, the people of Bahrain, may continue to devote our resources (and our minds) to its glory and that we may, to some small extent, redeem a portion of the debt we owe it.

It is clear from both the ancient and the modern history of our region that God has ordained that in order that our nation may survive, we must be animated by a noble warrior spirit. Strength is one of the essential requirements of a state whether in its purpose, its structure, or its defensive capabilities. It should be strong in leadership, in its economy and in the use of technology, as well as in its sciences, arts, literature and laws. God exhorts us to be strong: 'Against them make ready your strength to the utmost of your power, including steeds of war to strike terror into the hearts of the enemies' (Sura Anfal V60). Deterrence has always been and continues to be an essential national strategy.

Strength in the service of justice is a requirement of both individuals and nations: 'A strong man of faith is better and dearer to God than a weak one.'

Everyone can serve the cause of national defence according to the degree of his resources and abilities, for we have much to defend: 'One who fights without material resources is a martyr; one who fights for his property is a martyr; and one who fights for his honour is a martyr.'

The power which God has ordained us to develop must continuously evolve in order to keep pace with scientific and technological progress. We need to develop scientific knowledge and apply it wisely in order to progress. It requires enlightened minds and determined spirits to carry civilization forward. A nation is strong when its people are imbued with faith in their religious and cultural heritage, as well as confidence in their own abilities. Only in this spirit are we able properly to defend ourselves.

The region has witnessed many crises and conflicts engendered by foreign forces in their struggle to gain hegemony over it. These dangers will never subside as long as these elements continue to covet us, and hence there is no alternative to creating a competent and effective Arab military force to defend the development of our region and its resources. This is the real meaning of co-operation and the common destiny of the various states. It will enable us to reduce and avoid dangers. The Defence Force is only an exemplary aspect of our discharge of our sacred duty towards the motherland. Our hopes and expectations are pinned on it. It has the honour of defending the country and protecting values, heritage and independence so that it may inspire confidence, and its citizens enjoy security and stability.

In view of Bahrain's geographical and demographic limitations, and in order to face the challenges we have mentioned, we have to follow a policy of self-reliance after placing our trust in God. We must select effective modern weapons which can offset the deficiency in manpower. It requires constant training for our armed forces organized in small self-contained combat groups capable of confronting an enemy effectively. This should enable us to carry out a general mobilization, taking into consideration the integrated military co-operation among GCC states within the framework of Arab collaboration.

Our holy struggle in God's cause should be the essence of this military strategy. We should try to achieve a comprehensive civilizational renaissance in all its varied expressions in every Arab and Muslim country, benefiting from the lessons learned from the past in coping with the vital issues of the day which particularly affect our destiny. Our region forms the eastern wing of the Arab nation whose security is indivisible and this requires constant alertness in its defence.

This is the main reason for my dwelling on the importance of the Defence Force, and for giving this account of its inception and some of my modest experience in this field, although we are still at the beginning of the road. This is reflected in the title of this book 'First Light' – that is, in military parlance the advent of a new day which brings the opportunity for fruitful achievement.

To illustrate the purpose of this book I have briefly drawn on my own first experiences in choosing military service and then in developing the Defence Force. I have outlined its aims and our experiences with it, leaving the details to the accounts of individual commanders.

Since no good work can be completed without joint, dedicated efforts, I thank all those officials and advisers who participated in the preparation of this book.

I wish my colleagues in the service of our nascent state all success and prosperity as travellers in the same boat. God alone is our guide along the right path.

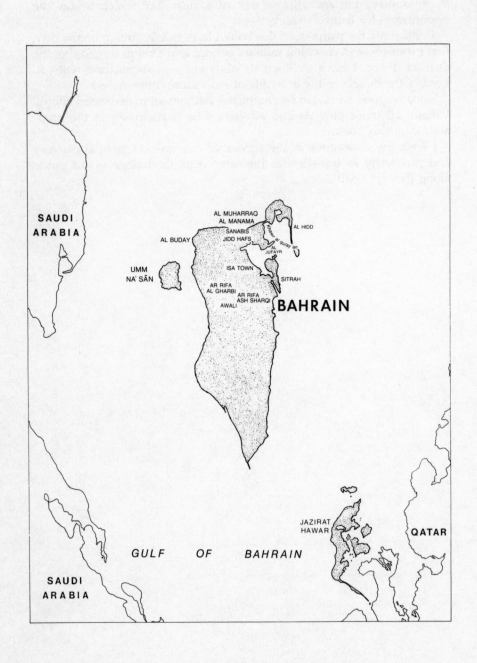

SAUDI
ARABIA

SAUDI
ARABIA

UMM
NA' SĀN

AL MUHARRAQ
AL MANAMA
SANABIS
AL BUDAY
JIDD HAFS

AL HIDD

Khawr al Qulay'an

AL
JUFAYR

ISA TOWN

SITRAH

AR RIFA
AL GHARBI
AR RIFA
ASH SHARQI
AWALI

BAHRAIN

JAZIRAT
HAWAR

QATAR

GULF   OF   BAHRAIN

A Brief Geographical and Historical Survey

The Arab Gulf lies between the Arabian Peninsula in the west, Iran in the East, the Strait of Hormuz and the Gulf of Oman in the south and Iraq in the north. The length of the Gulf is about 430 nautical miles and its width varies from 160 nautical miles at its widest to 21 nautical miles at its narrowest point which is at the Strait of Hormuz. In view of the depth of its bays which are suitable for anchorage, its calm waters and navigability, it became an important maritime centre. Its shores attracted the establishment of various settlements and forts throughout history.

The Arab Gulf abounds in islands and the most important of them are the islands of Bahrain. Bahrain is made up of an archipelago consisting of a total of over 33 islands forming a rough triangle. To its west and north-west lies the Kingdom of Saudi Arabia, to the north the Arab Gulf and to the east and south the State of Qatar. The total area of its territory is 687 square kilometres. Its population is approximately 531,000.

The Arab Gulf region had always been and still is in one of the important regions of the world from its geography and natural resources. Its location makes it a bridge between the East and West and with a strategic position between the Indian Ocean and the Mediterranean Sea, facilitating contact between Asia, Africa and Europe. It is given added importance by its natural resources of oil and mineral wealth. This has caused it to be coveted by the great powers through the ages. Since the dawn of history, the Gulf region was subjected to the attacks of greedy adventurers. Its shores have witnessed a succession of civilizations such as the Semite Sumerians, Akkadians and Babylonians.

1

Its waters have been the scene of long periods of conflict between the East and West with a series of military expeditions. Alexander of Macedon and his army traversed the Gulf region on their way to India and the Far East. Similarly the region was subjected to continuous wars between the Sassanids and the Byzantines which ended in the downfall of both empires at the hands of the Muslim Arabs in the wake of the Islamic conquests in the seventh century AD. Then the colonialists came to dominate the area and established military bases for the protection of their economic interest. Colonialism has since withdrawn never to return.

These factors to which the Gulf region was exposed especially affected Bahrain because of its strategic location at its centre. It has an abundance of sweet water, agricultural resources and a variety of food. Ships had to pass by Bahrain through various periods of history for the replenishment of water, food and fuel. Bahrain was also surrounded by a number of pearl-banks which made it famous. This was described by several historians and shown in the maps of the region. Travellers and sailors eulogized them in graphic detail. Virtually every historian or travelwriter who passed through Bahrain, whether an Arab or outsider, mentioned the pearl-banks and the way the pearls found their way to the markets of the East and West to be sold for fabulous prices. This and other reasons led the invaders and colonialists to impose their control over Bahrain since earliest times.

While I do not wish to go deeply into history, I would like to draw a certain conclusion from the history of our country. In brief this is that Bahrain so continuously faced challenges throughout long periods that this became its natural and habitual reaction. Its civilization was rooted in the need to face a continuous challenge in the shape of wars or battles which it fought on its own soil with courage, patience and faith, while assimilating all elements that were new into its own formation. Interaction with other cultures left indelible impressions on Bahrain. The melting of elements of various civilizations into a single crucible imparted a quality of adaptability to its society and contributed to its finer development.

As Bahrain was subjected to a great many confrontations, its people learnt many lessons in the art of warfare and the defence of their land. It became an article of faith with its people, wherever they were, to acquit themselves honourably in this role. I shall briefly review some aspects of heroism displayed by our forefathers as recorded in history and describe their noble character. These epics have been narrated and handed down by earlier generations to our own. The reader of modern history may wonder how Bahrain, with such a limited territory, could protect its position and actually benefit from playing a balancing role between the larger contending forces. The answer is to be found in its wise and courageous leadership and its expert use of weapons. These were the main reasons for success. Mere bravery cannot produce results without weapons. Similarly, weapons alone are not enough without their skilful use. This principle applied in the past to the sword and the spear just as later it applied to muskets, guns and rockets.

History tells us how in the middle of the eighteenth century various Arab tribal representatives gathered in Zubara around Mohammed bin Khalifa the Great, whom they accepted as their leader when they became aware of his outstanding character and qualities and his mature wisdom and piety. His rule was benign and he honoured their scholars. He established mosques and schools and built a fort named the Marir Fort for their protection. When his son Ahmed assumed the leadership after him, they persuaded him to build fortifications and towers around all entrances to the fort. They contributed the necessary funds for the purpose. He started to implement the proposal so that his forces might have a well-fortified defensive position to foil his enemies. The people had great confidence in their leader in whom they discovered a deep knowledge of warfare and qualities of wise leadership gained from experience and the inheritance of his father's fine traits of character. History tells us that the rule of Ahmed had not lasted long when the army of Nasr Al Madhkur, the ruler of Bahrain at that time, advanced on Zubara. He was driven by jealousy and hatred because the people of Zubara enjoyed peace, stability and progress and were rich and prosperous.

Ahmed and his followers rallied in defence of the country. Their fort, with its twelve defensive structures, constituted a formidable barrier for the aggressors. Ahmed then proved his outstanding leadership and skill in combat. By virtue of his courage and initiative, the forces of his enemy Nasr were crippled. Nasr fled to another country to save his skin, leaving his home and people to the mercy of Ahmed. Ahmed, at the head of his forces, at once proceeded towards Bahrain not to take revenge on the people who had come against him or to destroy their property, but to prepare the way to peace and stability throughout Bahrain and rebuild it.

In this he was guided by the character of the Holy Prophet, may peace and blessings be upon him, as he showed his sublime conduct when he told the people of Mecca after conquering it: 'Go, you are free, and today is the day of mercy.' Inspired by this Islamic spirit of tolerance and guided by traditional Arab ideals, Ahmed entered Bahrain in 1783 AD. Its people gave him a hearty welcome, and gathered under his banner to build with him the modern Bahrain.

History has recorded that Ahmed showed a noble, high-humanitarian attitude when the family of Nasr Al Madhkur pleaded with him to be permitted to go and join Nasr in the place to which he had fled. He ordered that the family be transported by ship to that country with all honour and dignity.

Since then the country has faced a number of invaders during the past two centuries but throughout this period the people of Bahrain rallied to their rulers and faced the enemies with great heroism and determination. Several battles took place in which they made glorious sacrifices. History could record for posterity the extent the present signs of civilization and prosperity around us owe to their armed struggle against the invaders.

In the following chapters we review the aspects of Bahrain's military history in modern times.

The Military History of Bahrain in Modern Times

CHAPTER 1

Bahrain, Islam and Foreign Invaders

A From the Advent of Islam to the Portuguese Invasion

The Arabs gave the name 'Bahrain' to the entire coastal length of the apex of the Arab Gulf in the north (including Kazima) to Oman in the south. It included the islands adjacent to the Arab Gulf coastline which were then known as the Awal Islands. This regional name was applied until the middle of the thirteenth century when the term began to be applied more specifically to the group of islands now known as Bahrain, although the entire area continued to be loosely referred to as 'Bahrain' for centuries afterwards. The biggest island was then called Awal which was the name of the deity worshipped by the Wa'il tribe of Adnan. This was the tribe which mingled with the other Arab tribes of Bahrain around the fourth century AD.

At the time of the advent of Islam, Bahrain was rich in agricultural wealth, in view of the fertility of its soil, its plentiful water resources and its location along the coast. It was populated by such tribes as Abdul Qais, Tamim, Bakr Bin Wa'il and Al Azd. Al-Blazeri recalls that when he was in Bahrain before Islam he found there a larger population of Arabs. Mundhir Bin Sawa Al Tamimi was their governor and it was he to whom the Holy Prophet wrote a letter inviting him to join Islam or pay the *jizya* tax. The letter was sent through Al-Ala Bin al-Hadhrami in 8 AH/630 AD. Mundhir accepted Islam as did all other Arabs and some non-Arabs who were there. However, there were some others such as the Magians, Jews and Christians who opted to pay the *jizya* tax which was accepted.

7

The text of the Holy Prophet's letter to Mundhir Bin Sawa ran as follows:

> In the name of God, the Merciful the Compassionate.
> From Muhammad the Prophet of God to Mundhir Bin Sawa.
> Greeting to you. Praise to God and there is no God but He I bear witness that there is no God save Allah and Muhammad is His servant and prophet. I remind you of the mighty and glorious Allah. The advice is tendered to one for his own sake. One who obeys my messengers and follows their instructions obeys me. Those who proffer advice to them advise me. My messengers have spoken well of you and I commend you to your people. Leave those of your people who accept Islam in their positions. Those among them who have sinned in the past are forgiven, so accept them. As long as you continue in your good work you will not be removed from it. Those who remain Jews or Magians shall pay Jizya.

The Holy Prophet sent Al Ala Bin al-Hadhrami to Mundhir Bin Sawa Al Abdi at Bahrain with a letter as follows:

> In the name of God, the Merciful, the Compassionate.
> From Muhammad the Prophet of God to Al Mundir Bin Sawa.
> Greetings to one who accepts guidance. I invite you to Islam, so accept Islam and be delivered. Accept Islam and God will continue you in your possessions. Know that my religion will spread in all corners.

Mundhir Bin Sawa replied to the Prophet accepting Islam and affirming his fealty: 'I read your letter to the people of Hajar. Among them are those who loved and appreciated Islam and entered its folds even as some of them despised it. In my land there are Magians and Jews on whom your orders have been enjoined.'

Thereafter the Prophet sent another letter to Mundhir Bin Sawa. The text is as under:

> In the name of God, the Merciful, the Compassionate.
> From Muhammad the Prophet of God to Mundhir Bin Sawa.
> Greetings in the name of God. Praise to God and there is no God but He. One who accepts our Qibla (direction in which prayer is offered) and partakes of our sacrificial animal is a Muslim. What is in our favour will be in his favour and what is against us will be against him. One who does not accept it shall pay a dinar in terms of *Maafiri* [the then current coinage]. Greetings and God's mercy. May God grant you forgiveness.

In this manner Bahrain peacefully joined the community of Islam during the time of the Prophet of God. The Holy Prophet sent Aba Hureira along with Al-Ala Bin al-Hadhrami. Al-Ala sent to the Holy

Prophet considerable sums of money contributed by the pious people of Bahrain.

The Holy Prophet transferred Al-Ala to another part of Bahrain – al-Qatif – and appointed Aban Bin Saeed Bin al-Aasi Bin Umayya over another part. It is said that the Prophet dismissed Al-Ala and appointed Aban in his place. When the Holy Prophet passed away, Aban left Bahrain and went to Madina. Then the people of Bahrain requested Abu Bakr (the Prophet's successor) to return Al-Ala to them. Abu Bakr accordingly restored Al-Ala who remained the governor of Bahrain until he died in 20 H. His grave is well known and located at Ras Ali on the western coast of the Arab Gulf.

After the death of the Prophet, several retrograde apostate movements against Islam sprang up in various parts of the Arabian island. When Mundhir Bin Sawi passed away in the same year in which the Holy Prophet died, that is 11 H, the offspring of Qais Bin Thalaba turned their backs on their faith along with Al Hatam. But later the tribe of Banu Abdul Qais returned to Islam. Al-Ala had then left Bahrain for Madina but he returned at the head of an army and killed the leader of the apostate movement, Al-Hatam. It is said that Khalid Bin al-Waleed was the one who killed Al-Hatim in 11 H, and it was at that time that the people of Bahrain requested that Al-Ala should remain their governor. It was in this manner that he liquidated apostate movements against Islam.[1]

During the Caliphate of Omar, Abu Hureira became the spiritual and temporal head in Bahrain in 17 H. Al-Ala Al Hadhrami then led an expedition against the Persians although Caliph Omar had forbidden him to venture on a sea campaign. He led a large fleet of three groups of ships across the sea from Bahrain to the Persian coast and landed at Astakhr. The Persians under the leadership of Al-Harbasa surrounded the attackers and cut them off from their ships. With the enemy in front and their backs to the sea they had to fight and in this battle many of the great Muslim commanders fell – among them Al-Sawar Bin Hammam and Al-Jarood Bin al-Moalla. Since their ships had been sunk they had to make their way to Basra by land. But the Persians, under the leadership of Shahrak, had cut off their route. When Caliph Omar learnt of this, he dismissed Al-Ala and wrote a letter to Ataba Bin Ghazwan asking him to send help to the Muslim soldiers and link up with Saad Bin Abi Wiqas. Omar reinforced them with 12,000 troops brought by Ataba Bin Ghazwan who fought the Persians and defeated them. They returned with a lot of booty and thus the very first seaborne expedition by Muslims was launched from Bahrain.

Othman Bin Abil Aas al-Thaqafi, the governor of Bahrain, later conquered Astakhr in Persia. He sent a strong army eastwards to India and

Sri Lanka during the reign of Caliph Omar Bin al-Khattab. During the time of Othman Bin Affan, Astakhr once again rebelled and the governor of Bahrain sent his brother Tamim Ibn Abil Aas who subdued Astakhr and killed its king Shahrak. Then Saboor, Kazeroon and Janaba were conquered.

Bahrain remained the base for eastern conquests during the period of the Rashidoon (rightly-guided) Caliphs and also during the reign of the Omayyeds when Bahrain was affected by the apostate movement of the Kharijites. In 67 H Najdat Bin Omar al-Hanafi advanced against Bahrain. The Bahraini people resisted but the Kharijites subdued them by force. The reasons for the resistance of the people of Bahrain (Banu Abdul Qais) to the Kharijites were as follows: (a) Tribal instinct – the Kharijites depended on the Bani Haneefa and Bani Bakr Bin Wa'il and hence the Banu Abdul Qais opposed them. (b) Local feeling – Bahrain resisted them in order to preserve its independence although it was plagued by internal divisions. The Omayyed state at the time faced various problems which led to the success of the Kharijites in Bahrain.

When Abdul Malik Bin Marwan sent an army to subdue the Kharijite Abi Fadeek in 73 and 74 H, it overcame him and put him to death. However, the Kharijite movement reappeared in 86 H, and prevailed over Bahrain for nineteen years. Thereafter, it was overwhelmed by the power of the Omayyed state.

During the Abbasid period Bahrain faced several movements, among them the Zenj revolt in which the Zenj leader imposed a tributary tax on the people of Bahrain and forced their allegiance to him until he was killed in 270 H, and Bahrain returned to Bani Al Abbas.

Thereafter Bahrain faced the Qarmatian Movement in 287 H, which subdued Bahrain and the surrounding areas until Amir Abdulla Bin Ali al-Ayouni was able to uproot the Qarmatians. Bahrain then remained under the Ayounis.[2]

The Ayouni state in Bahrain (including Al-Hasa, Al-Qatif and Al-Bahrain) was established in 468 H/AD 1074, and continued until 636 H/AD 1238. It was established in Bahrain itself by Abdulla Bin Ali Mohammed Bin Ibrahim al-Ayouni and the other Ayounis from the tribe of Abdul Qais.

After the Ayounis, Bahrain had two sets of rulers who each lasted about 150 years: first, the Bani Asfoor and then the Al Jabur. The Asfoor and Jabur are names which are sometimes applied to the offspring of the Bani Amer who are traced to Uqail Bin Amer.

The rule of the Al Jabur in Bahrain began in the late eighth century of Hijra and their kings included Ajwad Bin Zamil and Muqrin Bin Ajwad Bin Zamil who crushed the Portuguese but was fatally wounded in battle. The Al Jabur continued to govern Al-Hasa until the Ottomans established their rule in the tenth century of Hijra.

B   The Portuguese Invasion and its Lessons

The fifteenth century AD was marked by several major events which brought about great changes in the history of the world. In the east the Ottoman Turks won sweeping victories on the soil of Anatolia. Sultan Mehmet the Conqueror occupied Constantinople in AD 1453 and as a result its scholars scattered all over Europe. In the West, Arab rule ended in Spain. However, the Arabs enriched the sciences in Europe and their scientific influence continued to be felt for many decades after they left Andalus.

In AD 1492 America was discovered by Christopher Columbus, and the whole century is regarded as the great age of European geographical discoveries.

After the failure of the successive assaults of the Crusades, the Islamic world continued to pose an obstacle to Europe in its march towards the East. Hence Christopher Columbus turned west in order to discover a new route to India. In AD 1498 Vasco da Gama of Portugal undertook a voyage along the west coast of Africa and around the Cape of Good Hope towards India. This voyage marked the entry of Europeans into the Islamic waters east of Africa and the Indian Ocean. The Red Sea and the Arab Gulf were now threatened by the ambitious Europeans who hungered for the domination of Islamic trade routes and the wealth of the East. The Portuguese spearheaded this new colonial onslaught.[3]

The Portuguese considered themselves soldiers of the Crusades in their onslaught on Islamic lands. They instigated the Negus of Abyssinia to fight against the Muslims and they planted the symbol of the cross over government buildings on the island of Hormuz. Their leaders wrote letters to the King of Portugal in which they proudly announced the burning of the lands of the infidels (Muslims) and the cruel rape and torture of their population.[4] They also revealed their plans to attack the Islamic shrines in the Hejaz.

The Portuguese primarily aimed at establishing colonies in India to use them as launching-pads for other objectives. They were able to establish these bases during the course of seven years in various parts of India such as Goa and Cutch. From here they started making preparations to implement their subsequent plans to secure places which dominated and controlled Molucca in the east, Hormuz at the entrance of the Arab Gulf and Aden at the entrance of the Red Sea.

The Invasion of the Gulf

In their Goa colony in India, the Portuguese made the necessary preparations for the invasion of the Gulf. Alfonso de Albuquerque was appointed to conduct this expedition in AD 1506. He was one of their most aggressive and influential men. The King of Portugal's instructions to Albuquerque were that his main task was to close the entrance to the Red Sea in order to deprive the merchants of Egypt of their Far Eastern trade and to establish Portuguese sovereignty over the entrance to the Gulf at Hormuz in order to control Arab maritime trade with the Far East and India on the one hand and shipping from the Red Sea and East Africa arriving in the Gulf on the other. Hormuz occupied a key strategic, political and commercial position at the eastern corner of the Arabian Peninsula.[5]

Albuquerque began his attack on the coasts of Oman in AD 1507 with the aim of destroying Omani shipping wherever it was found. Under his leadership, a regular naval force which was well equipped – especially with artillery – carried out fierce destructive attacks with fire and pillage.

The Portuguese were able to occupy Qalhat, Sohar and Khor Fakkan, until they reached Ras Musandam from which they could raze Hormuz. At the beginning of the sixteenth century AD, the Arabs of the eastern coast of the Arabian Peninsula and the Gulf were haphazardly organized under the flags of various local leaders. It was increasingly difficult to form a disciplined force to confront the regular foreign forces equipped with the latest weapons. In general the Portuguese were launching their attacks against Islamic countries at a time when these were riddled by internal weakness and division. The kings or rulers of each region, and sometimes individual towns, plotted against each other, and tried to expand at the expense of his neighbour.[6]

The Ottoman empire had not yet extended to the Gulf region. However, the Ottomans established their sovereignty over Syria and Egypt in AD 1517, and with this the young Muslim state was able to dominate the traditional caravan routes of the Arab East. The Ottomans continued their advance by occupying Iraq and then expanding southwards towards the areas of the former Islamic Caliphate. In order to confront this newly emerging power and because of the prospect that it would clash with Persia, the Westerners plotted to attract the Persians to join them.[7]

The Kingdom of Hormuz adopted strong defensive measures to confront the expected Portuguese attack and it was joined by the Bahraini fleet for the plan of battle. The Portuguese fleet advanced from Ras Musandam and attacked Hormuz. After a bloody battle Albuquerque was victorious and it was agreed that tribute would be paid to the Portuguese. Hormuz was also forced to recognize the authority of the Portuguese crown.

The reinforcements which were sent by Bahrain to Hormuz included men and supplies. The Portuguese laid an ambush for them in the waters of the Island of Kishm. In the bitter fighting which ensued the Portuguese were successful and sank the Bahraini ships.[8]

Albuquerque then returned to Goa, after arranging a tripartite agreement between himself, the Persian Safavid state and the Kingdom of Hormuz. In India the King of Portugal appointed in place of Almeida a new viceroy who started preparing for other naval expeditions in the Gulf and the Arabian Sea.

The southern part of Iraq was under the control of the Safavid state. In 920 H/AD 1514 the Ottoman Turks overcame the Persians in the battle of Galdiran and the northern part of Iraq as far as Baghdad came under the rule. This caused the Safavid state to increase its co-operation with the Portuguese. The Arabs of the Gulf and the Muslims of India had looked upon the Ottomans as their liberators from the calamitous threat of the Crusades represented by the Portuguese. In India and the Gulf, resistance to the Portuguese intensified and the Ottomans began to rig up a naval fleet to fight the Portuguese. An Ottoman fleet unexpectedly arrived in the Indian waters to assist the Muslim rulers. As the Portuguese threat of invasion of the southern Gulf began to dwindle, Albuquerque was spurred to seek the permission of the King of Portugal to advance this time in the direction of Aden and the Red Sea to cut the routes of the Ottoman fleet.[9]

In AD 1513, Albuquerque advanced with his fleet to Aden so that from there he could launch himself through the straits of Bab al-Mandab into the Red Sea according to the directive of the King of Portugal. This expedition failed miserably in spite of its repeated attacks on Aden. Albuquerque returned to Goa and sent another expedition under his nephew Piro to the entrance of the Gulf which plundered some Arab trading vessels. In the end this expedition was forced to turn back near Hormuz and Piro returned to Goa in AD 1514.

Invasion of Bahrain in AD 1521

Bahrain was the focus of Portuguese attention in view of its important strategic location at the heart of the Gulf and its abundant orchards, date-groves and pearl-banks. The Portuguese had chosen it as the depot for the merchandise of Syria and the Arabian Peninsula. It nominally owed allegiance to the King of Hormuz to whom it paid an annual tribute.[10]

According to the evidence of the Portuguese, the most important population centre in Bahrain was the city of Bahrain which was surrounded by a wall made of stone and lime and contained a huge, impregnable fortress.

After the failure of Albuquerque's expedition against Aden and the Bab al-Mandab straits his attention was again attracted to the Gulf. The first attempt to invade Bahrain was in 917 H/AD 1511 by Khwaja Attar, the uncle of the King of Hormuz, and Turan Shah, who had been appointed by the Portuguese. He found a pretext in the refusal of Muqrin, the ruler of Jabur in Bahrain, to pay the income from his orchards to Hormuz as had been agreed. He alleged that Muqrin intercepted the ships which sailed between Hormuz and Basra. In addition to the coveting of the agricultural riches and pearl-banks of Bahrain by the King of Hormuz,[11] the Portuguese had started plundering Bahraini ships before the attack by Khwaja Attar. He faced severe resistance from Jabur and was forced to return to Hormuz without success. Another Portuguese attempt by an expedition of four ships under Albuquerque's nephew Piro also failed. After this the Portuguese started preparing for a decisive battle with Muqrin.

General situation

The Portuguese and their allies in Hormuz started preparing their naval expedition to destroy the opposition of Bahrain by occupying it and liquidating the state of Jabur which had become a threat to their influence through the reputation which King Muqrin enjoyed. The invading forces were assembled in Hormuz and the Portuguese commander Antonio Corea was appointed commander of the expedition. It included 3,000 Persian and Arab mercenaries carried in 200 ships and led by Rais Sharaffuddin of Hormuz. The Portuguese forces was made up of 400 men carried in 7 ships equipped with heavy guns.

The king Muqrin al-Jabari started reinforcing his defences. He constructed a strong embankment 10 feet wide, reinforced with stone and lime and fronted with palm trunks. He sited the guns on the walls and in the openings of the towers. He also dug deep trenches at appropriate places along the coast to form a considerable depth of defensive positions from the coastline to the main defence in the port and the adjoining areas behind the embankment where the invasion was expected. Finally, he divided the defensive front into sectors, each with its own commander in well situated positions. These measures showed that he was a military commander with a clear strategy.[12] The only place which was suitable for the landing of troops was the port of Bahrain. (It is believed that the fort stood in front of the town on the sea and dominated the port.) Muqrin was able to mobilize 12,000 Arab soldiers, 400 archers and 300 Persian Arabs with 20 Turkish soldiers equipped with guns in charge of training. These forces were deployed at key points with a special concentration before the wall of the fort to meet the enemy.

On 15 June AD 1521, the Portuguese invasion forces approached Bahrain and deployed in battle formations in front of the fort. Antonio Corea waited six days for reinforcements, which had been dispersed by bad weather, to join him.

The guns of the Portuguese ships were new and of heavy calibre. They had an overwhelming superiority in fire-power over the defenders. But Muqrin and his forces were fully prepared for battle; they had confidence, high morale and grim determination.

The battle

In the first phase, Corea landed part of his forces to establish a foothold on the coast. This attempt failed in the face of fierce resistance from the defenders, and the Portuguese were forced to withdraw by wading out to their ships at low tide.

In the second phase the heavy Portuguese guns concentrated their fire on the fort itself and the defensive positions parallel to it. The Portuguese landed their forces far away from the fortifications but the forces of the Kingdom of Hormuz were told to remain aboard the ships until ordered to disembark. Heavy fighting broke out between the attackers and defenders. The latter concentrated their forces within the walls of the fort. Corea was urging the soldiers to stay and storm the fort, but their efforts failed. Muqrin was in the forefront of the defenders bearing the brunt of the attack with great courage and chivalry, inspiring his soldiers until he was badly wounded in his leg. Antonio Corea was also wounded in the arm.

The battle continued for a few days more and the Portuguese soldiers were bored by the lack of decisive results. Fate decided that Muqrin

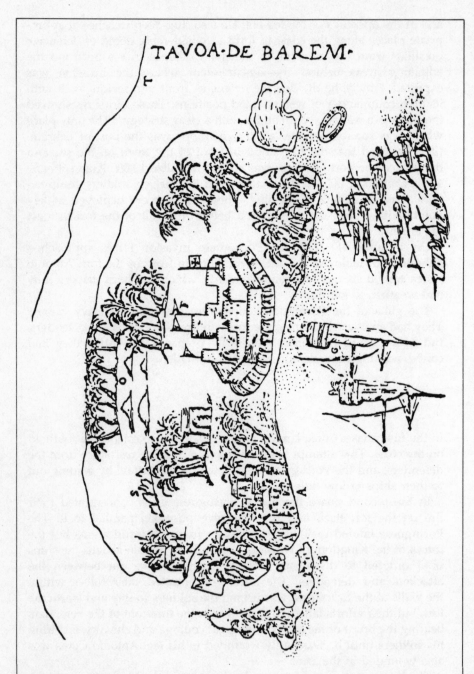

TAVOA·DE BAREM·

Figure 1 A Portuguese map of Bahrain as seen from a distance, showing the Bahrain fort as drawn by Go de Castro in AD 1538.

should die a few days after he was wounded. The loss of their leader immediately lowered the morale of his men. This, in turn, raised the morale of their enemies. The remaining soldiers of Hormuz also joined in to mop up the defenders and pursue them. Hameed, a nephew of Muqrin, assumed command of the Bahraini troops and ordered them to withdraw to Qatif. They were carrying the body of their amir Muqrin for burial in Al-Hasa. The losses on both sides in men were high as severe fighting continued for a number of days. The losses of the defenders were greater after their leader Muqrin was wounded as it reduced their will to resist. Some of them surrendered. The island was occupied and pillaged and its ships set on fire.

Lessons learnt

1 Offensive action and initiative

The Portuguese, during their operations in the Gulf region, held to the twin principles of offensive action and initiative. They were constantly on the offensive even though they were fewer in numbers than the defenders during the invasion of Bahrain. But they relied on their modern force which was superior in other ways that made them capable of applying these principles. They came from their own lands with the sole aim of launching an offensive to seize the treasures of the East. They were well versed in naval warfare and their assaults on the islands and coastal fortifications resembled operations of piracy in their use of terror tactics and swift manoeuvre. The leader who continuously maintains the principle of offensive action will be able to impose his will on his enemy. He will anticipate the reactions of the enemy and plan ahead.

2 Superiority in weaponry

The invading forces, particularly the Portuguese ships and their sailors, had superior modern weapons. The Portuguese wore protective armour which was not available to the defenders who had no previous experience of fighting a modern European naval force. Superior weapons give a decisive advantage to the party which possesses them even against a larger opposing force. It also weakens resistance and the will to fight. This is what happened in the war between Italy and Abyssinia in 1936 in which Italy used poison gas against the Abyssinian forces and, despite their stubbornness, brought the war to a speedy conclusion. A similar example is the use of atomic weapons against Japan in 1945 which put an end to the Second World War.

3 *Leadership*

Both sides had good leadership. Leadership is the most important element in achieving decisive results and winning a war. If Muqrin had not fallen in battle, perhaps the results would have been different. A leader himself, however competent will not suffice in a critical situation. This leads us to the logical conclusion that one should always provide for one or two commanders of high calibre ready to assume immediate responsibility under unfavourable circumstances.

4 *Morale*

This is another important factor in war and the major elements behind morale are good leadership and strength of faith. In the beginning of the battle the morale of the defenders was very high and remained so as it was sustained by the grim determination of their leader Muqrin, but it suffered later when he was wounded and left the battlefield. This caused the defenders to lose heart; they suffered heavy losses and some of them surrendered.

5 *Other factors*

The division and weakness which prevailed in the eastern shores of the Arab Peninsula helped the invaders to isolate individual countries so that no one helped another. Had they been able to group together to ward off the Portuguese danger, events would have followed a totally different course. There would have been a co-ordinated effort with the launching of surprise attacks and naval ambushes against the Portuguese forces whenever the opportunity arose.

The Portuguese force did not rely on the element of surprise in its invasion of Bahrain. The arrival of the force in separate groups to the shores of Bahrain as a result of stormy conditions at sea prevented the application of the principle of the concentration of force. If the defenders had had the means, such as long-range artillery or the elements of a naval force, to engage the enemy as they approached in dispersed formations, they would have caused serious casualties in their ranks even before they reached the coast. This could have foiled their plans.

Revolt against the Portuguese

The people of the Gulf resisted Portuguese domination and never submitted to it. The first violent uprising took place in 928 H/AD 1521 under the leadership of the King of Hormuz, Shah Bandar. This uprising wiped out the centres of trade and commerce in the Gulf in Hormuz,

Correia Barém

Figure 2 Muqrin Bin Zamil al-Jabari, ruler of Bahrain, was martyred in AD 1521. His head is shown mounted on the shield of Portuguese commander Antonio Corea (based on Portuguese sources).

Bahrain, Muscat and Sohar during the single night of 30 November 1521. The revolt was largely successful in Bahrain where it was led by the governor. He rushed into the fort against the Portuguese, arrested the Portuguese ruler of the island, hanged him forthwith on a date-palm and banished the remainder of his soldiers. Thus the direct Portuguese influence over Bahrain was ended. In Hormuz the Portuguese ships in the port were burned and their military garrison on the island liquidated, the Arab ships attacked several Portuguese positions in the Gulf and a large number of them were taken prisoner.[13]

Successive Portuguese reinforcements from India were sent to quell the revolt. The first reinforcement, followed by another in quick succession, arrived in 929 H/AD 1522 under the leadership of Dom Louisie Veneris. Muscat was overcome, Sohar was destroyed and the Hormuz revolt liquidated.[14] But in Bahrain the Portuguese used mild diplomatic tactics and concluded an agreement with the governor of the island. They confirmed him as the ruler of Bahrain on condition that he would include a Portuguese adviser/assistant in his government.

In 93 H/AD 1526 fresh revolts broke out in Hormuz, Muscat and Qalhat but these were soon suppressed. These years later the people of Bahrain started a violent uprising which deserves mention in some detail. Destruction, killing and cruelty were the hallmarks of Portuguese conduct in their operations in the Gulf from the outset. Their main aim was to plunder the resources of the country and conspire against the Islamic faith. Therefore, there were many successive revolts against them until they reached a stage of utter exhaustion. The immediate reason for the revolt in 1529 was the exaction of additional taxes by the Portuguese from the people of Hormuz. They tried to pass on some of the burden to Bahrain, but the latter refused. The Portuguese viceroy in India, Nunoda Cunha, then organized a naval expedition to attack Bahrain, and appointed his brother Simon to command the force which was to be reinforced with contingents from Portugal. Simon first proceeded to Hormuz, and in September 1529 advanced towards Bahrain with five ships carrying 400 Portuguese soldiers. These were followed by a few local ships. This force approached Bahrain Fort and bombarded it for three days, but the ruler of Bahrain and the defenders of the coastline and fort held out steadfastly until the attackers had exhausted their ammunition. The Portuguese were unable to inflict any appreciable damage on the walls of the town. In the end, the Arab ruler of Bahrain offered them a conditional peace which they declined. They were, in fact, looking for plunder and booty. They waited fourteen days for the return of a ship which had gone to bring more ammunition from Hormuz.

During this fortnight a fever epidemic broke out among the ranks of the invaders which sapped their will for battle. Their food supplies had run out and they started seeking food from the Arabs who did not deny their request according to the true spirit of Islamic tolerance and traditional Arab hospitality. Ultimately the attackers decided to withdraw without a single gain. On their way back most of the remaining Portuguese died, including the leader of the expedition, Simon da Cunha. Perhaps his death may be attributed to the ignominious defeat he had suffered.[15]

Entry of the Ottomans against the Portuguese

The Arab and Ottoman reaction against the Portuguese intensified in the Red Sea, the Arabian Gulf and the Indian Ocean. The mobilization of internal forces clearly assumed a national dimension in the form of a warning to the people of the region of the dangers of Portuguese designs. However, this national reaction had no immediate and effective results at first because of the Portuguese superiority in weapons and the lack of a strong political power to meet the Portuguese challenge. There were no means of equipping a naval force equal to the enemy.[16] The Portuguese continued to be the undisputed rulers of these waters during the first three decades of the sixteenth century. Later, the Portuguese rulers of various colonies indulged in a life of luxury and comfort. In the beginning their leaders were endowed with great determination. They were equipped with superior weapons, had better organizational skills and were dedicated soldiers. These qualities started gradually to decline, particularly when the leaders and other senior officials turned to making money through trade.

Of even greater importance was the appearance of a new and strong opponent of the Portuguese in the Ottoman state which had gained control over Egypt in 1517. Thereafter, it annexed Yemen and in 1534 the Ottomans occupied the city of Baghdad and started advancing southwards in the direction of the Gulf.

The Mameluke state in Egypt had staged successful naval expeditions for the protection of the Red Sea from the Portuguese danger before the Ottomans entered Egypt. The Ottomans' arrival in Egypt and the extension of their authority to other Arab countries gave the Ottoman state the additional responsibility of defending Islam as a unified, political and military power, and of confronting the Portuguese.

Portuguese sources point out that the King of Al-Hasa and the ruler of Bahrain were then independent and they both sent delegations to Baghdad when it fell in 1534, to convey their felicitations and greetings to the Ottoman Crown Prince although they did not owe any allegiance to him. That was the first contract between Bahrain and the Ottoman state. The Ottomans referred to this event as the oldest legal basis[17] for their title to Bahrain.

The Ottoman state became a powerful empire in the sixteenth century with its fleet in the Mediterranean. It was capable of launching its fleet from Suez along the Red Sea and the Arabian Sea as far as the Gulf. After the fall of Basra in 1546 to the Ottomans, the waters of the Gulf came within easy reach for their naval operations. The first major naval agreement between the Ottomans and the Portuguese took place when a fleet sent by Sultan Sulaiman al-Qanooni through the Red Sea under captain Peri Mohiuddin Rais, who was known as the Captain of Egypt, sailed in the direction of the Gulf in 958 H/AD 1551 along with a large force of soldiers in about 30 ships.[18]

The appearance of this fleet gave a shock to the Portuguese. Peri attacked Muscat, captured it and arrested its Portuguese commander along with his garrison. Afterwards he attacked Hormuz and captured it while the fort remained under the control of the Portuguese. Then he proceeded to Qishm and occupied it. Later he captured a lot of booty from Basra, and hurriedly returned on learning that the Portuguese were concentrating their naval force to waylay him. He returned with three ships loaded with booty and plunder which he had captured from the Portuguese in Oman. One of these ships sank within sight of Bahrain and finally the Sultan ordered Peri's execution for his behaviour.

After the occupation of Basra by the Ottomans in 1546 they advanced towards the Gulf coast by way of Shatt al-Arab and Al-Hasa which sought their help against the tyranny of the Portuguese. In response, they sent a military garrison to Qatif. There was continuous contact between the Arabs of Al-Hasa, Bahrain and the Ottomans.

About the middle of the sixteenth century many naval encounters took place between the Ottomans and the Portuguese in which the former suffered defeat in some engagements due to the small size of their fleet and also the serious lack of co-ordination among the Islamic ports to deal a decisive blow against the Portuguese.

Between 1550 and 1562 Turkish naval attacks continued against the Portuguese and the Turks scored several victories. They destroyed the Portuguese in Qishm and twice entered Muscat in triumph. They also landed in Hormuz and bombarded it. In 1559 the Turkish fleet consisting of 2 warships and 70 sailing boats reached Bahrain. This force inflicted losses on the Portuguese in naval battles but failed to achieve its aims. The Ottoman documents state that Murad, the governor of the island of Bahrain, had declared his allegiance to the Ottoman state, and had been appointed ruler of Bahrain, but the governor of Al-Hasa, Mustafa Pasha, committed aggression against Bahrain in 966 H/AD

1559 in his individual capacity. Sultan Sulaiman al-Qanooni therefore dismissed him and appointed Morad Bik in his place. The Sultan offered to strengthen the friendly ties between the Ottoman state and Bahrain and to secure its shores against further Portuguese invasion. The Ottoman documents refer to the defeat of the force despatched by the governor of Al-Hasa which was surrounded and disarmed by the Portuguese. This force was withdrawn to Al-Hasa in accordance with the terms of reconciliation agreed between the two parties which included a huge sum to be paid as tribute to the Portuguese.[19]

The Portuguese forces started withdrawing from the Gulf in 1580 when Spain annexed Portugal to its territory for a period which lasted sixty years. Severe blows were then directed against Portuguese power in the Arab west. In the battle of Wadi al-Makhazin which took place close to the city of Al-Qasr al-Kabir in the north of Morocco in 986 H/ AD 1578 the King of Portugal Don Sebastian was killed and the Moroccan forces totally destroyed the Portuguese army.[20] Relations between the Persians and the Portuguese weakened considerably towards the end of the sixteenth century and in 1581 Turkey launched an expedition against Muscat under the leadership of Ali Bik. He overran the Portuguese Fort in a surprise attack by land and sea and the Portuguese garrison fled to the interior of Oman. Then the Arabs ambushed the Portuguese in Nakhiloo in 1585; more than 250 Portuguese troops were killed. Others fled towards their ships. This was the biggest single blow to the Portuguese invaders.

Expulsion of the Portuguese from Bahrain

The people of the Gulf were resolved to end the cruel treatment and terror tactics of the Portuguese, the plunder of their wealth and control over their trade. They were waiting for an opportunity to rebel against them. In 1602 a Bahraini stabbed the Portuguese governor of Bahrain to death and declared himself the ruler. The people of Bahrain stormed the fort and overran the Portuguese garrison. The Portuguese era in Bahrain was drawing to its close.

The Portuguese desperately tried to recover Bahrain by grouping their forces and those of Hormuz and summoning reinforcements from India, but their efforts were doomed. An epidemic broke out among their soldiers. Shah Abbas of Iran sent a force of 5,000 men to Bandar Abbas to divert the attention of the Portuguese; a revolt broke out against their garrison in the port. As a result the Portuguese were unable to move against Bahrain.[21]

Lessons learnt from the Portuguese invasion

The invaders intended to establish Portuguese supremacy over the trading centres of the Arab Gulf. The Portuguese came to impose themselves through the use of terror. They displayed the bigotry of the Crusaders against anything even remotely connected with Islam. The Portuguese practised naval piracy, and intercepted every ship passing through the Gulf waters to plunder its cargo. The following conclusions may be drawn from the history of the Portuguese in the Gulf over a period of about 100 years:

1 Blockade

The primary objective of the Portuguese was to prevent the Arabs from trading with India and the Far East. They attacked Arab ships wherever they were in order to immobilize them. In this way they tried to achieve their commercial and military goals. The military aim took precedence after they had achieved a measure of stability in the Gulf so that none of the states could either singly or jointly oppose them. From his first arrival in the Gulf in 913 H/AD 1507, Albuquerque destroyed every ship which he met en route. He would set on fire the ships which had put into various Gulf ports; and this included even those vessels which played no role in war. Whatever commercial vessels survived this onslaught had to obtain the formal permission of the Portuguese to set sail. This one way of establishing their control over the sea routes which they strengthened by establishing a number of military garrisons and other fortified bases in the region.

2 Local resistance

Popular resistance to the Portuguese hegemony started to manifest itself here and there, and continued to strengthen in spite of the local dissensions which then prevailed. We have seen how the rulers and citizens of some countries staged violent rebellions and how in due course these developed into mass movements. The revolt of 1522 under the leadership of the King of Hormuz was the first co-ordinated uprising against the Portuguese in Hormuz, Bahrain, Muscat and Sohar.

The ambush which was laid in Nakhiloo and which led to the death of 250 Portuguese was a glorious example of mass resistance. The uprisings and resistance had a tremendous effect on the Portuguese and their morale.

3 State power and strategic aims

The strength of the Portuguese and their superiority in weapons derived from the power of their state which constantly sent reinforcements of regular troops to the theatre of operations and continued pursuing its aim even when some battles were lost. The Portuguese were far superior to local forces in the Gulf. However, when the Ottoman state entered the scene of battle and suffered some initial reverses, their nascent state took them in their stride and continued to prepare fresh attacks. They resolutely pursued their aim until they created panic among the Portuguese. Soon they started scoring victories over the Portuguese and the people of the Gulf began to look to the Ottoman state as an Islamic power and custodian of the two holy shrines. Hence they were ready to co-operate with it fully.

The main reason for the success of the Portuguese in the initial stages of their campaign was the absence of a strong and unified state power to oppose them. The only state which was capable of doing this was the Ottoman empire which, during the first half of the sixteenth century, was busy strengthening its foundations and extending its authority over the Arab territories of Egypt, the Fertile Crescent and the Arabian Peninsula. It commanded strong naval forces in the Mediterranean. After the occupation of Egypt in 1517, and Basra in 1546, the Ottoman naval forces began vigorous operations in the Red Sea, the Arabian Sea and the Arab Gulf. They operated from two bases – one in Suez and the other in Basra. Therefore, the Ottoman naval operations against the Portuguese appeared to come from two directions and this greatly increased the power of their impact.

4 Alliance with the Safavid state
In certain periods some local rulers collaborated with the Portuguese who were able to exploit the long-standing disputes between the Safavids, the Ottomans and parts of the Gulf. An agreement between the Portuguese and the Safavids was therefore effective. This is the sort of policy that foreign powers have pursued in the past and still do today to create conflicts between Iran and the Arab Islamic countries. If Iran had stood against the Portuguese during the Arab revolts against them in the Gulf and during the Ottoman confrontation with the Portuguese, the position of the invading forces would have become extremely precarious and they would have been unable to remain in the Gulf region as long as they did.

C British Role in the Gulf

The struggle between the Ottomans and the Portuguese in the latter half of the sixteenth century increased in intensity, while at the same time the conflict continued to rage between the Ottomans and the Persians. While some of the Ottoman naval expeditions against the Portuguese were at first unsuccessful, they later started registering successes. The real value of the Ottoman operations against the Portuguese lay in the fact that they were aimed to seize the initiative. The second half of the sixteenth century also saw British and Dutch attempts to place obstacles in the path of the Portuguese in India and the Far East.

In 1598 the first British delegation to the court of the Shah Abbas of Persia, offered to reorganize the Persian army on a modern basis and to work for the establishment of a closer relationship with the Christian West.[22] The aim of this move was to widen the gulf between the Ottomans and the Persians to serve the future imperialist ambitions of the British and help them to act against the Portuguese whose power and influence were on the decline. In 1609 the British East India Company established its first centre at Surat in India. British influence started spreading from there towards the Arab Gulf. The British alliance with Persia was directed against the Ottomans and the Portuguese, and they were able to obtain special trade facilities. The hatred of the people of the region for the Portuguese helped the development of relations with the British and gave it a sense of purpose.

In 1602 the Portuguese were expelled from Bahrain by its people who were followed by other peoples of the Gulf, particularly the Yaariba of Oman. By 1622 the Portuguese had lost Hormuz and Qishm and been chased out of every port in the Gulf. Finally, they were turned out of their own fort in Qishm through a joint operation in which a strong force of Shah Abbas, supported by British ships, attacked the Portuguese fleet and the fort in Hormuz which fell in April 1622. The Portuguese flag was unceremoniously lowered from the fort after a period of fourteen years.[23] The surviving 3,000 Portuguese soldiers stationed in Hormuz were taken prisoner. A close alliance was formed between the British and the Persians. The Persians bore the brunt of the battle of Hormuz in which they lost about 1,000 men while British casualties were only 20 wounded. The British had already broadened their interests in Persia and established agencies in Shiraz and Isfahan and elsewhere.[24]

The last of the Portuguese were in Muscat, Oman. They tried to form an alliance with the Turks against the British and Persians. With this aim they established a trading centre and Portuguese settlement in Basra to divert Portuguese trade to this city. A limited military alliance

developed between the Turks and Portuguese, which launched successive attacks against the Persian coast in an attempt to prevent the Arabs
of the northern Gulf from allying themselves with the British and Persians in the south. The combined Turkish and Portuguese naval forces in
the northern Gulf, however, were not powerful enough to overcome the
Anglo-Persian alliance.

The Portuguese suffered their final blow in Yemen where the Yaariba
state was established. The remainder of them were expelled when the
Muscat Fort fell in 1650. Those who remained in Basra became mercenaries.

References

1 Al Blazeri: *Futooh Al Buldan*, pp. 106–7, Egypt, 1957; *Bahrain through the Ages*, vol. 1, p. 125, Bahrain, 1983. Al Najam: Abdul Rahamn Abdul Kareem, *Al Bahrain Fi Sad Al Islam*, p. 101, Baghdad, 1973.
2 Sinan, Mahmood Bahjat, *Al Bahrain Durratul Khaleej*, pp. 59–62, Baghdad. (It is said that Caliph Omar dismissed Aba Huraira because he was too lenient and spent all his time at prayer.) See *Al Aalam* – Zarkali 80/4, and *Bahrain through the Ages*, op. cit., pp. 119–29.
3 *Al Watheeka*, January 1984 – Ahmed Al Anani, 'The Portuguese in Bahrain and the Surrounding Areas', p. 77; Dr Aba Hussain, (Pages from the History of Portuguese Influence in Bahrain), *Al Watheeka*, No. 1, 117, July 1982.
4 Dr Ahmed Bu Sharab, 'The Contribution of Portuguese Sources and Documents in the Recording of the History of Bahrain during the First Half of the Sixteenth Century', *Al Watheeka*, No. 4, p. 118.
5 Hormuz was an Arab kingdom which was established on the islands of Qishm and Jeron. It flourished as a commercial centre at the entrance to the Gulf with close links with the Persian mainland.
6 *Al Watheeka*, No. 4, p. 86.
7 Dr Ahmed Bu Sharab, op. cit., p. 118.
8 *Al Watheeka*, No. 1, 128; and no. 4, p. 90.
9 *Al Watheeka*, No. 4, p. 85.
10 The Royal Central Asian Society Magazine for 1935, Part 22, p. 618, London.
11 For further information see *Al Watheeka*, No. 3, pp. 95–8; and No. 4, pp. 76–100.
12 Dr Ahmed Bu Sharab, op. cit., p. 118.
13 *Al Watheeka*, No. 3, pp. 95–8; and No. 4, p. 96–9.
14 *Al Watheeka*, No. 4, p. 118; and No. 1, p. 138.
15 Al Sairafi, Nawai Hama, *The Portuguese Influence in the Arab Gulf*, pp. 140–3, Riyadh, 1983.
16 Ibid.
17 For more details, cf. *Al Watheeka*, No. 4, pp. 98–100.

18 *Al Watheeka*, No. 4, p. 101; and No. 1, pp. 142–3.
19 *Al Watheeka*, No. 4, pp. 101–2.
20 Sairarfi, op. cit., p. 146; and *Al Watheeka*, No. 4, p. 63.
21 Ottoman document – Ahmed Asrar: *Religious Policy of the Ottoman State during the Period of Al Qanooni.* Another unsigned Ottoman document says the writer was a witness to all that happened to the Turkish force in Bahrain in 1559, and the actions of the governor of Al Hasa, Mustafa Pasha, who invaded Bahrain without the permission of the Sultan. See *Al Watheeka*, No. 1, pp. 146–8; and No. 4, p. 108.
22 Dr Al Tazi Abdul Hadi, 'An Unpublished Document about Bahrain', *Al Watheeka*, No. 4, pp. 58 and 109.
23 *Al Watheeka*, No. 4, pp. 108–12.
24 *Ibid.*, No. 4, pp. 109–16.

CHAPTER 2

The Battle of Zubara and the Transformation of Bahrain

A   Bahrain in the Eighteenth Century – Al Madkhur and Al Utoob

After the final exit of the Portuguese from Bahrain at the beginning of the third decade of the seventeenth century, the country was ruled by some Arab tribes inhabiting the Eastern coast of the Gulf. Occasionally they paid tribute to Iran. The best known of these tribes was Al Madhkur which ruled over Bahrain in the middle of the eighteenth century until the siege of Zubara which took place in 1197 H/ 1783 AD. This siege ended in failure and Shaikh Nasr Al Madhkur immediately fled to Bushire. The Utoob then entered Bahrain.

Al Madhkur

Al Madhkur are said to belong to the Al Nusoor who were the Haula Arabs from Matarish in Oman. Others say they came from the tribe of Bu Mahair of Nejdi Arabs who were settled in Bushire from 1056 H/ 1646 AD.[1] They lived in some ten villages on the eastern coast of the Arab Gulf, with their greater concentration in Qavandia and Kankoon. Among those from the Al Nusoor tribe who achieved fame was Shaikh Jabara who ruled over Kankoon and Kung to the east of the port of Linga. His rule extended to other areas[2] such as Tahiri which was a famous Arab port known as Siraf and enjoyed commercial importance due to its position in the centre of the Gulf on the sea-route to India,

Sarandib (Sri Lanka) and the Far East. Bahrain was under the influence of the Imam of Muscat until 1131 H/AD 1718 when Shaikh Jabara conspired with the Persians against the Imam who then withdrew from Bahrain. Shaikh Jabara started paying tribute to Persia, but he had already begun to rule over Bahrain some time before 1143 H/AD 1730, according to Dutch documents. He was a contemporary of Shaikh Rashid Bin Matar al-Qasimi, the ruler of Basidu, and co-operated with him. Shaikh Jabara's rule lasted until 1150 H/AD 1737, when Nadir Shah of Persia established his authority over Bahrain. He asked Shaikh Jabara and Shaikh Rashid to crush the rebellion which had been launched by Ahmed al-Madani in the south of Persia, but because they were lax in carrying out his orders, Nadir Shah occupied Bahrain. However, Shaikh Jabara laid siege to the Bahrain Fort in 1151 H/AD 1738, and recovered control.

On the death of Nadir Shah in 1160 H/AD 1747, Persia lost its control over Bahrain. Shaikh Nasr Al Madhkur became ruler of Bahrain until the time of Karim Khan Zand of Persia to whom he was forced to pay an annual tribute, fixed at 4,000 tomans. On this condition he was allowed to continue to rule over Bahrain.[3]

In due course the tribe of Al Haram who came from the Al Houla who used to rule Asaloo, occupied Bahrain.

However, the Shaikh of Bushire, Nasr Al Madhkur, and Shaikh Mir Nasir, the ruler of Bandariq, combined in 1165 H/AD 1751 against the tribe of Al Haram and they jointly occupied Bahrain.

Shaikh Mir Nasir later took over as sole ruler of Bahrain which forced Shaikh Nasr Al Madhkur to leave Bahrain for Bushire as he no longer received his share of revenues. Shaikh Nasr Al Madhkur tried to return to Bahrain after concluding an alliance with the Utoob.

However, Nasr Al Madhkur failed in the face of resistance from the Haramis and the remnants of the tribe of Houla in Bahrain. So he approached the Al Nusoor (the House of Nasr) in the fort of Tahiri for assistance. Shaikh Nasr Al Madhkur occupied Bahrain in 1167 H/AD 1753 when the Haramis withdrew to Asaloo.

Shaikh Nasr and his brother Saadoon Al Madhkur remained as rulers of Bahrain. We see the name of Saadoon mentioned as the ruler of Bahrain in 1175 H/AD 1761 in contemporary Dutch documents.[4] In 1191 H/AD 1777, Karim Khan Zand ordered Shaikh Nasr Al Madhkur, now ruler of Bushire and Bahrain, to subdue Zubara and occupy it. Shaikh Nasr tried but failed in this expedition because of the fierce power struggle then taking place in Persia. This weakened the expedition because Shaikh Nasr was involved in these events. However, Shaikh Nasr tried several times to subdue Zubara which was ruled by Shaikh

Ahmed Bin Mohammad Al Khalifa of the Al Utoob during the period 1193–1195 H/AD 1779–1781 but could not succeed.[5]

Shaikh Nasr Al Madhkur enjoyed great influence and considerable wealth; he owned several trading vessels which sailed to Muscat and India. He had a special armed force to guard his ships and property. When he died he left much wealth which was inherited by his son, who was also called Nasr. Persian influence was restricted to the collection of tribute which was sometimes not paid when conditions in Persia were disturbed as happened on the death of Karim Khan in 1193 H/AD 1779.

In 1197 H/AD 1783 Shaikh Nasr Al Madhkur attempted a full-scale invasion of Zubara and besieged the town. When the siege failed and the battle was lost the Al Madhkur fled to Bushire in Persia. This became known as the 'Fall of the Nusoor' and marked the beginning of an era of the Al Utoob in Bahrain. Following the defeat and flight of Shaikh Nasr, Shaikh Ahmed Bin Mohammed Al Khalifa turned his attention towards Bahrain and conquered it in 1197 H/AD 1783. He became known as Ahmed al-Fateh – or 'the Conqueror'.

The Utoob

The tradition is that the Utoob were a branch of the Jumaila Wa'l clan who were famous in Nejd in Central Arabia, living in Aflaj and Hadder near Wadi Al Dawasir. Remnants of them may still be found in this region.

The migration of the Utoob from Nejd in the ninth decade of the eleventh century of Hijra, i.e., between AD 1671 and 1680. They settled down in Qatar for about 33 years. During this period they were able to respond to their new environment and acclimatize themselves to sea-faring, pearl-diving and maritime trade along with other peoples of the Gulf. Competing with them in these fields gave rise to jealousy and disputes. They fought bitter battles against their enemies in those shores and some migrated to Basra in 1113 H/AD 1701. After a few years these moved to settle in Kuwait.

The Utoob were a group of inter-connected tribes bearing this name. They established their village settlements on the Qatar coast, and were referred to as the Utoob tribe. Other tribes undoubtedly mingled with them but they constituted the core.

There were several migrations from Nejd of other individuals and groups who established village and town settlements but they were not closely-knit like the Utoob. For example, the Zubair came predominantly from Nejd but were not from one clan. They were made up of several households and families. The Utoob, however, were closely integrated

31

through intimate ties from the start of their migration. They were referred to in history as the Utoob tribe and individual members of the tribe referred to themselves as "so-and-so al-Utubi'. They had a common slogan and war-cry of 'Aalad Salim' (i.e. 'Sons of Salim').

At the beginning of their migration the Utoob were neither as numerous nor as strong as they subsequently became. When other individuals, tribes, families and clans joined them their numbers increased and they became powerful.

An Ottoman document of 1113 H/AD 1701 states that when those of the Utoob and their followers migrated to Basra they constituted 200 families in 150 ships with guns and each carrying about 40 musketeers. We could thus estimate their number as 10,000 including their families and followers. This was a substantial number for those days.

The oldest historical reference to the Utoob found so far is a document of 1112 H/AD 1700, titled *The Two Pearls of Bahrain* by Yusuf Bin Ahmed Dirazi. He mentions a battle in Bahrain in which the Utoob were involved.

The other historical proof of the presence of the Utoob in the Gulf generally and in Bahrain in particular is contained in the Ottoman document obtained from the Ottoman Prime Minister's Archives. It is in the Register of Important Documents No. 111, page 713, describing the events of 21' Rajab 1113 H/December 1701 when the Utoob visited the Governor of Basra.

Some time after 1113 H/AD 1701, they went to Grane (Kuwait) where there was a fort which had been converted into a garrison by the ruler of Al-Hasa and Qatif, Ibn Orai'an al-Khalidi, for the protection of the northern borders of his state. He granted the fort to the Utoob who made a settlement around it at the beginning of the twelfth century of Hijra/eighteenth century AD.

Shaikh Khalifa Bin Mohammed, the ancestor of the Al Khalifa, built the famous mosque in Kuwait, known as the Al Khalifa mosque, and endowed it with part of the date corps from the orchard he owned in Qatif.

Around 1120 H/AD 1708 Shaikh Khalifa Bin Mohammed died and was buried in Kuwait. He was succeeded by his son Shaikh Mohammed Bin Khalifa who was still an adolescent and hence remained under the care of his uncle Shaikh Sabah Bin Jabir who gave him his daughter in marriage. A son Khalifa was born to them. We infer from this that Shaikh Khalifa died before his son Mohammed Bin Khalifa was married and that when Mohammed was married and blessed with a son he named him Khalifa after his father according to the prevailing custom. This supports the saying of the late Shaikh Abdullah al-Salem al-Sabah, Amir of Kuwait, that the Al Sabah and the Al Khalifa, when they first settled in Kuwait, shared a single kitchen because of the intimate bonds between them.

With the passage of time Kuwait expanded and bustled with activity. Its population increased in view of its special advantages such as a harbour with excellent anchorage for ships, its commercial location and proximity to pearl-banks. The Utoob unanimously selected Shaikh Sabah Bin Jabir as their ruler.

We do not support the statement of some who claim that Kuwait was founded in 1125 H/AD 1713[6] or the assertion of Warden that the Utoob first inhabited Kuwait in 1128 H/AD 1716.[7]

A document exists which shows that the first judge of Kuwait was Shaikh Mohammed Feiroz (d. 1135 H/AD 1722).[8] Certainly the town would have been established much earlier. We estimate that it was established before 1120 H/AD 1708 and that it was previously known as Al-Qurain (or Grane) which later became Kuwait.

The Dutch documents give us, in a report written by Kniphausen, Director of the Dutch East India Company in Kharag, and his assistant John Hulst in 1170 H/AD 1756 a description of the coastal region of the Gulf and its population. The report had been forwarded to Jacob Mosel, Governor-General of the Dutch East India Company. The following appears in this report about the Utoob:

> Shaikh Nasser Al Madhkur sought shelter with the Utoob and requested their help in conquering Bahrain and in return promised them exemption from paying any tax for pearl-fishing in the pearl-fisheries of Bahrain. The Utoob excelled in diving.

This is the first mention of the Utoob in this report which goes on to describe the various harbours and shaikhdoms of the Gulf. The report continues:

> After Euphorias (Fao) comes the island of Vaginae on the Arab coast and Grane is located opposite Vaginae. These places are inhabited by the Arab tribe of Utoob who are affiliated to the Shaikh of the Bani Khalid tribe to whom they pay a meagre tribute. They have 300 ships, most of which are small, which they use for pearl-diving. This is their sole means of livelihood when the rains are scanty. They number around 4,000, and are equipped with swords, shields and spears. They are not familiar with guns and are always at war with the Arabs of the coast in a state of perpetual enmity.
>
> However, the size of their ships does not permit them to venture long voyages.
>
> The pearl-banks which they visit for pearl-fishing are between Bahrain on the one hand and Ras Bardistan near Congon (Kankoon) on the other.

Although they have many tribal shaikhs, nevertheless they live in amity, the important ones among them being Shaikh Mubarak Bin Sabah and Shaikh Mohammed Bin Khalifa.

In a report written in 1213 H/AD 1798, it is stated that Grane (Kuwait), Zubara and Bahrain belonged to the Arabs of the tribe of Bani Utoob and that these places were united under one government at the head of which were Ahmed Bin Khalifa, the Shaikh of Bahrain, and Abdullah Bin Sabah, the Shaikh of Grane. Both the shaikhs were men of strong character and dedication, who exerted themselves to the utmost for the welfare of their respective tribes. They had earned the respect and loyalty of the general public in the gulf. The Utoob had become the most powerful among the sea-faring Arabs with a substantial number of ships which carried merchandise between Muscat and Basra. The governments of Grane, Zubara and Bahrain were worthy of respect for their adherence to strict standards of justice and in this regard they could be compared to the government of Muscat. Foreigners who visited these ports and resident merchants enjoyed total protection.[9]

The Utoob certainly used to frequent the Gulf ports in the course of diving operations, commerce and transhipment of merchandise.

The Bin Ali clan who were a part of the Utoob migrated from Kuwait to Fureiha in Qatar and settled down there around 1145 H/AD 1732. They were the matrilineal uncles of Shaikh Ahmed Bin Mohammed Al Khalifa who bore the title 'Al Fateh' or 'The Conqueror'.

Some other Utoob, including the Al Khalifa, also migrated to Qatar and Shaikh Mohammed Bin Khalifa established the township of Zubara in 1762. He had five sons. They were Khalifa, Ahmed, Muqrin, Ibrahim and Ali.[10]

Those were not the days of passports and landing permits. All ports were open to incoming and outgoing passengers. Customs duties were also unheard of. There, however, were places where the merchants paid a percentage tax.

B Zubara

Zubara is a town situated on the north-western coast of the Qatar peninsula. The word 'Zubara' in Arabic is derived from Zabar meaning the layer of stones one over the other. The people of the Gulf take it to mean a mound or small hill. This township was named Zubara because of the presence of a small mound in the site. There is also another place in Qatar with the name Aba al-Zubar.

In naming the various parts of their desert, the Arabs used suggestive

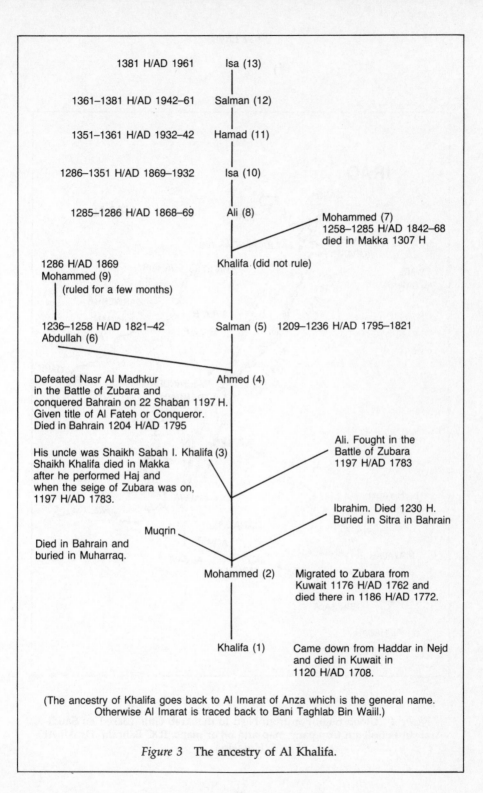

1381 H/AD 1961   Isa (13)

1361–1381 H/AD 1942–61   Salman (12)

1351–1361 H/AD 1932–42   Hamad (11)

1286–1351 H/AD 1869–1932   Isa (10)

1285–1286 H/AD 1868–69   Ali (8)

Mohammed (7)
1258–1285 H/AD 1842–68
died in Makka 1307 H

1286 H/AD 1869
Mohammed (9)
   (ruled for a few months)

Khalifa (did not rule)

1236–1258 H/AD 1821–42
Abdullah (6)

Salman (5)   1209–1236 H/AD 1795–1821

Defeated Nasr Al Madhkur
in the Battle of Zubara and
conquered Bahrain on 22 Shaban 1197 H.
Given title of Al Fateh or Conqueror.
Died in Bahrain 1204 H/AD 1795

Ahmed (4)

His uncle was Shaikh Sabah I. Khalifa (3)
Shaikh Khalifa died in Makka
after he performed Haj and
when the seige of Zubara was on,
1197 H/AD 1783.

Ali. Fought in the
Battle of Zubara
1197 H/AD 1783

Ibrahim. Died 1230 H.
Buried in Sitra in Bahrain

Muqrin

Died in Bahrain and
buried in Muharraq.

Mohammed (2)   Migrated to Zubara from
Kuwait 1176 H/AD 1762 and
died there in 1186 H/AD 1772.

Khalifa (1)   Came down from Haddar in Nejd
and died in Kuwait in
1120 H/AD 1708.

(The ancestry of Khalifa goes back to Al Imarat of Anza which is the general name.
Otherwise Al Imarat is traced back to Bani Taghlab Bin Waiil.)

Figure 3 The ancestry of Al Khalifa.

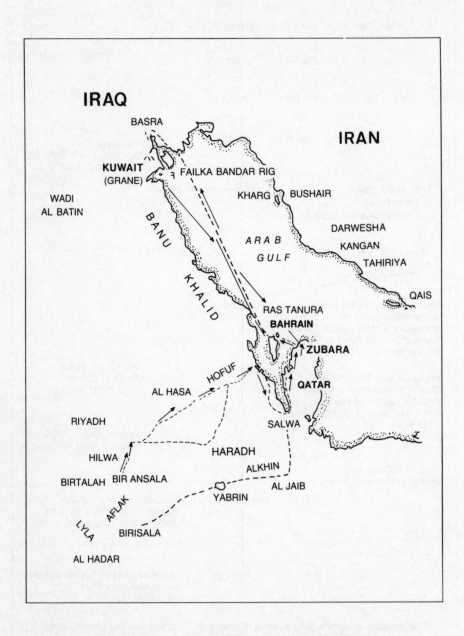

Figure 4 Utoob migration from Nejd to the Arab Gulf. (Based on Saudi Arabian Petroleum Company map and other maps; IDC Bahrain, Dr Ali Aba Hussain.)

words by which places could be identified. They selected Zubara to establish a settlement because of its proximity to a port with a good anchorage and the availability of water, with pastures and woods close by. Zubara is not mentioned in history before Shaikh Mohammed Bin Khalifa established it and built a famous fort in it after he had migrated from Kuwait to Qatar.

The explorer Niebuhr did not mention Zubara or show it on his map which he drew in 1179 H/AD 1765. Scarcely three years had passed since the establishment of the township of Zubara and it was practically unknown. Niebuhr drew his map a year before Shaikh Mohammed Bin Khalifa built the fort in Zubara. However, Niebuhr described other places in the Gulf such Grane and Qatar and in his map he refers to the village of Furaiha located near Zubara.

It was Shaikh Mohammed Bin Khalifa who established Zubara and brought it into history. The town developed and expanded and many people visited it because of its association with its founder and ruler Shaikh Mohammed Bin Khalifa and his sons who succeeded him and were all of high moral conduct, generous with a strong sense of justice and a capacity for leadership which enabled them to inflict defeat on their rivals until Zubara became the unrivalled capital city of both the Qatar peninsula and Bahrain.[11]

Zubara was probably established in 1176 H/AD 1762, and not in 1180 H/AD 1766. Shaikh Mohammed Bin Khalifa, after his migration to Zubara, married into the tribe of Al Bu Kawara and had two sons from this marriage – Ali and Ibrahim. Ali was one of the heroes of the Battles of Zubara and Bahrain in 1197 H/AD 1783 which means that Ali at the time would have been at most 20 years old if he was born around 1177 H/AD 1763. However, if the marriage of Shaikh Mohammed Bin Khalifa took place in 1180 H/AD 1766, Ali's age could not have been more than 16, and therefore he could not have taken a major part in the battle. On this assumption, the year of Shaikh Mohammed Bin Khalifa's migration to Zubara was probably 1176 H/AD 1762.

Shaikh Mohammed Bin Khalifa was the undisputed ruler of the town of Zubara and its people. He constructed a fort on a site where there was a source of water for the garrison and which was named Sabha. This was the name of the original fort in Hadder in Nejd. It was also known as the Marir Fort (Marir in Arabic means 'bitter', and referred to the water around which the fort was built). The pictures of the remains of this fort still remain. The building was fortified and the numeral analysis of Arabic letters yields the date of construction as 1182 H/AD 1768. Political and economic factors boosted the prosperity of Zubara and it expanded to become the largest town in Qatar.

Around 1186 H/AD 1772 Shaikh Mohammed Bin Khalifa died, and

was succeeded by his son Shaikh Khalifa. Shaikh Khalifa Bin Mohammed was a pious man and writer and poet. He was well versed in
'Fiqh' or Islamic jurisprudence as expounded by Imam Malik. Zubara's
further great expansion during his time is attributed to the following
reasons.

During the reign of Shah Karim Khan Zand, the Persians laid siege
to Basra for about a year and a half in 1188 or 1189 H. It is said that
the siege lasted 14 months until 1190 H/AD 1775–1776. The people of
Basra defended their town with superb courage despite the shortage
of food and ammunition.[12] Finally the Persians occupied Basra peacefully but then they stabbed the people in the back, plundered their
wealth and withdrew to Al-Zubair which they looted and left desolate.
The few who survived surrendered or were killed.[13] This led to the
flight of a number of wealthy and learned people from Basra and
Kuwait to Zubara, Al-Hasa and other southern areas because they were
safely remote from these developments. Basra was then a centre of trade
and brisk economic activity, and its prosperity had led to great progress
in culture and learning. So when a large number of merchants brought
with them their experience and wealth to Zubara, the town flourished
and prospered. A group of scholars, intellectuals and poets also settled
there and contributed to its educational advancement. They opened
several schools there on the lines of those in Basra. Both economically
and culturally Zubara prospered.[14]

Basra was then hit by a plague. An eyewitness to the events of 1186
H/AD 1772 was Abdul Rahman Bin Abdulla al-Suweidi, a contemporary historian. He moved with his family from Baghdad to Basra, then
to Zubair and lastly to Kuwait where he stayed for a month. He recalls
fourteen mosques there and two large ones for public congregations.[15]

Lorimer gives the date of these events as 1186 H/AD 1773. He states
that the plague killed about 200,000 people out of a total of 300,000 in
Basra.[16]

According to another account, very few people survived in Basra and
the estimated number of those who died of this disease was 350,000. In
Zubair 6,000 fell victim to the scourge. The epidemic drove many people
of Basra to Zubara and it was said that 'the desertion of Basra was the
building of Zubara'. Many *ulema* (religious scholars) who lived in
Zubara had previously lived in Basra for many years. They included
Bakr Bin Ahmad al-Basari al-Zubari who died in 1202 H, and his contemporary Ahmed Bin Darwesh al-Abbasi, Mohammed Bin Abdul Latif
al-Shafei al-Ahsai and his sons Abdullah and Mohammed Bin Fairooz,
Al-Baitushi, Al-Ateeqi, Al-Hajari, Al-Tabatabai, Ibn Jami' and others
who played a significant role in the cultural renaissance of Zubara.

At about this time the Al Saud and the reform movement of Shaikh

Mohammed Bin Abdul Wahhab appeared on the scene in Nejd as the authority of the Al Orai'ar weakened as a result of family feuds among them. So Amir Abdul Aziz Bin Mohammed Bin Saud established his authority of Nejd and the desert lands. This conflict led to the prosperity and economic progress of Zubara under the Utoob. Insecurity and instability, drove some of the people of Al-Hasa and Nejd also to settle in Zubara and Kuwait. The book *The History of Some of the Events Which Occurred in Nejd*, and also Ibn Bashr and Ibn Ghannam have confirmed that a great battle took place in 1187 H/AD 1773 along with several other incidents which caused Daham Bin Dawas Bin Abdulla Bin Sha'lan to leave Riyadh and make for Al-Hasa.

In 1188 H/AD 1774, Orai'ar Bin Dajeen Al Hameed Al Khalidi, chief of Al-Hasa and Qatif, together with a large force of troops from the urban and desert areas, advanced towards Nejd intent on taking Buraid and Onaiza and surrounded them. He drove some of them away, but while he was in action, he died and was replaced by his son Batin. He had hardly found his feet when his brother Saadoon strangled him. When Saadoon became ruler he fought the tribe of Mutair and in this he had the alliance of the Dhamisha from Anza. This situation persisted until 1195 H/AD 1780. These disturbed conditions in Al-Hasa and Nejd led to the departure of some of the people to Zubara, especially merchants and scholars.[17]

At the time when Zubara prospered and flourished there was famine and inflation in Nejd. In 1181 H/AD 1767 prices rose sharply in all parts of the region and the inflation continued during the following year. Consequently many people died of hunger and many more migrated from Nejd to Basra, Zubair and Al Hasa. The famine was followed by an epidemic of plague and then the wars until 1197 H/AD 1782 when an even greater famine and inflation occurred and lasted for three years.[18]

The arrival of the Al Khalifa and their followers in Zubara helped to generate wealth for its population due to their proximity to the main source of wealth in the Gulf which was the pearls. Zubara enjoyed a form of free trade. Because no duty was imposed on merchandise merchants were encouraged to flock there with their merchandise. It attracted a great quantity of consumer goods and the surplus went to Nejd, Al-Hasa, etc.[19]

Zubara also attracted a great deal of trade with Bahrain which at that time was under the rule of the Al Madhkur.[20] The prosperity, progress and wealth earned by the Utoobi ports of Zubara and Kuwait through their active participation in pearl-diving, the pearl trade and maritime transport aroused the jealousy of the Arabs of the coasts who started placing obstacles in their way and intercepting their ships. Rivalry between them hardened with the passage of time. Ali Murad Khan of Isfahan constantly encouraged the Arabs of the Persian coast to put an end to the rising Utoob power both in Kuwait and Zubara.

The Battle of Riqqa took place under these circumstances. After this battle, the Utoob from Zubara and Kuwait, who had joined forces, attacked Bahrain. A report written by Latouche on 4 November 1782, corresponding to 27 Zilqada 1196 H, and sent to his headquarters in London said:

> Some people of Zubara and Grane lately invaded Bahrain and captured a number of boats of Bushar and Bandariq at the entrance of the Shatt al-Arab river. Shaikh Nasr (Al Madhkur) gathered his forces from Bushire, Bandariq and other Persian ports and claimed that he wanted to avenge these acts of aggression by launching an attack on Zubara. So he sent a letter to Ali Murad Khan at Isfahan asking for his financial help to achieve his aim.[21]

At the same time, Shaikh Nasr of Bushire addressed a call to the Shaikh of Grane offering him peace between them, but the latter preferred to reject this initiative unless Shaikh Nasr agreed to pay him half the revenues of Bahrain and a large proportion of the revenues from Bushire. Not many years had passed since Grane had been obliged to pay a large amount of tribute to the Bani Kaab at a time when Zubara was hardly known.

At the time of the Persian attack on Basra one of the shaikhs of Grane moved to Zubara along with many well-known personalities and a number of merchants from Basra. Hence Zubara became a centre for the pearl trade and Indian goods. The importance of Grane as a commercial centre also increased to a certain extent. Late on, these shaikhdoms (Zubara and Grane) were able to challenge Bani Kaab and snatch several concessions from them because they were no longer afraid of threats from Shaikh Nasr. An analysis of the letter of Latouche quoted above shows that at the end of 1196 H/AD 1782, a strong dispute had arisen between the Utoob and the shaikhs of the Persian coast on the other, instigated by Ali Murad Khan. The reason was rivalry over the sources of riches such as pearl-diving, transportation through the sea, and retailing. This led to the outbreak of mutual raids.

The most reliable source of information about this is the above-mentioned letter written by Latouche dated 4 November 1782 corresponding to 27 Zilqada 1196 H, which states that prior to the date of the letter, the people of Grane and Zubara had staged an attack of Bahrain. Lorimer has stated that they inflicted a heavy loss on Manama and took away with them a ship which had come from Bushire. Latouche also mentions that some ships were sunk in the Shatt al-Arab by the Utoob and these also belonged to Bandariq, Bushire and the Bani Kaab. From this we may infer that these ships were the victims of the Battle of Riqqa in the vicinity of Failaka between the Utoob of Kuwait (Grane) during the reign of Shaikh Abdullah Bin Sabah, who ruled from 1171 H/AD 1757 to 1229 H, and the Bani Kaab and their allies. Latouche also stated that after this raid and victory on the river, the Utoob became so strong that they were no longer afraid of the Bani Kaab or Shaikh Nasr Al Madhkur. Only a short time before Grane had been forced to pay tribute to Bani Kaab, and Zubara had not yet achieved any fame. Now the Utoob of Zubara and Grane were no longer afraid of threats and, as mentioned by Latouche, Shaikh Nasr Al Madhkur claimed that he was going to invade Zubara and wrote a letter to Ali Murad Khan in Isfahan asking for his assistance.

At the same time he wrote to the Shaikh of Grane urging him to enter into an agreement with him but the Shaikh asked for half the revenues from Bahrain and a large proportion of the revenues from Bushire. It seems that his proposals for peace were merely a façade, because all he wanted was to create a division between the two allies, Zubara and Kuwait, so that the way would be clear for him to invade Zubara. He, in fact, completed preparations and launched his attack in 1197 H/AD 1783.

Lorimer as well as Latouche says that reacting to the events mentioned earlier, the ruler of Isfahan, Ali Murad Khan, gave orders at the end of 1196 H/AD 1782 for Shaikh Nasr Al Madhkur to surround Zubara with the assistance of the rulers of Bandariq, Janaba, Dashistan and others. The hard core of this attacking force was 2,000 men. It is well known that the strategist of this battle was Shaikh Nasr Al Madhkur himself. His sword fell into the hands of Salama Bin Saif Al Bin-Ali after his army collapsed and his forces were defeated. They withdrew to their ships after having suffered enormous losses. Shaikh Mohammed, the nephew of Shaikh Nasr Al Madhkur, was also killed.

Marir Fort

Marir Fort was built by Shaikh Mohammad Bin Khalifa in Zubara. Its construction was completed in 1182 H/AD 1768 on hilly terrain, about one kilometre from Zubara which was on land close to the sea. It was dominated by three towers, to the north, east and west. According to a visitor in that century, there were four towers in the fort equipped with artillery which was fired through various openings in the walls. Another witness measured the guns to be about 20 arm-lengths. They brought the guns from the coasts of Zanzibar through their friendship with its Omani ruler.

Inside the fortress there were about 50 houses for the commanders and their troops. The fort had a massive door on the north and a smaller entrance named 'Khadi'a' in the south. Near the main door there was a conference chamber and beside it a domed mosque. Inside the fort there was a fresh-water spring beside the mosque and three other springs outside the fort. The eyewitness account adds: 'During my last visit to the fort which was in 1350 H/AD 1930 I saw it intact except for the roof which had been destroyed. I saw guns near the fort and date-palms and a lotus plant on the southern interior. There were seats running the length of the inside of the fort.'

The route between the fort and Zubara was protected by two walls, one to the south extended from the gate of Zubara eastward towards the fort and the other northward from the door of the fort to the town door from the west. They also dug an elongated moat on the south side about two miles long, through which small ships could enter. This moat was lined by two walls extending from the town to the fort to protect the ships both inside and outside until they reached the fort which overlooked the entrance. Shaikh Mohammed Bin Khalifa was the man who dug this moat and built the two walls with towers protecting them. The foundation and walls of the fort were wide and strong.

A witness measured the width of the walls at the base as 5 arm-lengths (11 ft). The walls were high and it was named the Marir Fort (*marir* means bitter in Arabic), because the water of the spring inside, though fresh, was somewhat bitter.

In Qatar there was a fresh-water spring which was named *maliha* or brackish. Similarly, they named the fort Sabha or Sabeeha because of the view it afforded. It had been painted with gypsum and looked high, bright and white. It is said that the ancestor of the Utoob, Faisal al-Jameeli, had constructed a fort in Hadder in Nejd which he had named Sabha. Therefore when Shaikh Mohammed Bin Khalifa built this fort in Zubara he named it after the fort built by his forefathers in Nejd.

After Shaikh Mohammed Bin Khalifa completed the construction of the fort, he felt strong enough to stop payment of any tribute or tax to anyone.*

* Interviews with Shaikh Ahmed Bin Abdulla Bin Ahmed Al Ghatam who is nearly 100 years old, and Shaikh Jassam Bin Abdulla Al Khalifa, who is over 90.

Figure 5   Remains of Marir Fort.

C   The Battle of Zubara

Zubara prospered under the rule of Shaikh Mohammed Al Khalifa and became an established trade centre for pearls and Indian goods. Similarly, the commercial importance of Grane (Kuwait) also increased greatly. Both Zubara and Grane were able to challenge the Bani Kaab, and the Utoob became a powerful influence on events in the Gulf. Serious differences arose in the relations between them and the shaikhs of the Persian coast because of their rivalry for the sources of income such as pearl-diving, shipping and agency charges on the one hand, and on the other, the growing influence of the Utoob and their supporters in Zubara.

The friction that grew between them finally erupted into mutual raids. The Utoob of Zubara and Grane captured some boats belonging to Nandariq, Bushire and the Bani Kaab at the entrance of the Shatt al-Arab.[22] Similarly, the Utoob raided the island of Bahrain from Zubara on 9 September 1782, and attacked Manama after its ruler Shaikh Nasr sought refuge in the fort along with his forces. The document goes on to describe the details of this incident as follows:[23]

On September 9, the Utoob Arabs came from the Arab coast of Zubara

43

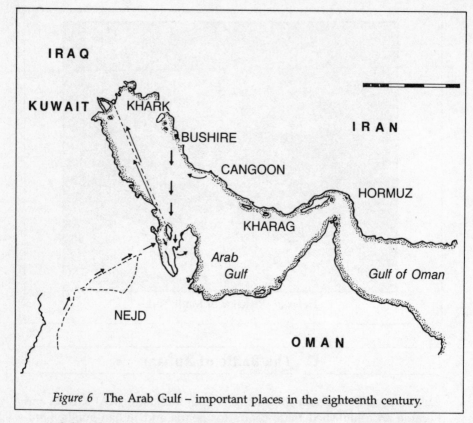

Figure 6 The Arab Gulf – important places in the eighteenth century.

and disembarked on the island of Bahrain. After a short battle in which both sides lost a number of men, they forced the ruler of the island, Shaikh Nasr, to withdraw to the fort. The attackers invaded the island forthwith and returned to Zubara on the third day. They took with them a galliot* belonging to Bushire which had been sent by Shaikh Nasr to bring the annual tribute from the island.

This news became known on 13 September and, on the orders of Ali Murad Khan, Shaikh Nasr commenced preparations for an attack on Zubara with the assistance of the shaikhs of Bandariq, Janaba and Dashistan located on the eastern coast of the Arab Gulf.

On 28 February 1783, a letter was addressed from Bushire to Bombay containing the following information about the preparations which Shaikh Nasr Al Madhkur was making for advancing towards Zubara:[24]

I informed you previously on October 5, 1782, about the attack on Bahrain

* Small transport sailing-boat with oars carrying about 40 men.

44

by the Arabs of Zubara in September. Now Shaikh Nasr is getting ready to proceed again Zubara on the instigation of Isfahan and he was collecting sufficient forces for this expedition until December 12. His fleet now consists of four galliots, 13 or 14 dhows* with accompanying boats and 2,000 men from Dashistan.

This force had started advancing towards Bahrain under the leadership of Nasr's nephew Shaikh Mohammed with the aim of forcing the Arabs to accept his terms by blockading their port. This would block their trade while the Persian fleet patrolled between Bahrain and Zubara. The Arabs do not have sufficient force to counter them so they made an offer through Mir Ghani, the ruler of Bandariq, that they were ready to return to Shaikh Nasr all the booty which they had captured from Bahrain if he was prepared to arrive at a peaceful settlement with them. When the mediation of Mir Ghani did not succeed, Shaikh Rashid, the ruler of Julfar, was given the task of mediating with wider powers to agree terms which would satisfy both parties.

The son of Shaikh Rashid reached here [Bushire] on December 23, 1782, carrying a letter from his father on the subject. It is expected that Shaikh Nasr will reach Bahrain during the course of the next few days and it is believed that there will be a peace agreement during the coming months.

The situation in the interior of Persia has not changed since I wrote last and peace prevails in Isfahan. It appears that the conduct of Ali Murad Khan has received the approval of the royal court. Murad Khan, the governor of Shiraz, sent a letter to the merchants of Bushire guaranteeing them full security and the non-imposition of any additional taxes on their merchandise.

The situation then deteriorated for these and other reasons.[25]

The reaction on the other side was that Shaikh Nasr started preparing his forces and his ships along with other necessary measures to launch an aggression against Zubara. He gathered a force from Bushire, Bandariq and the Persian ports and asked Ali Murad Khan of Isfahan for some money.

General situation

The chain of events described previously was the general situation prevailing between Zubara on the one hand, and Shaikh Nasr Al Madhkur on the other, during the period between September 1782 and the first half of May 1783. Grane stood by Zubara. After Shaikh Nasr had completed his preparations in December 1782, he launched the

---

* Sailing-ship common in the waters of the Arabian Peninsula and East Africa. A large war dhow was about 240 tons and carried more than 100 men.

expedition against Bahrain under the command of his nephew Shaikh Mohammed and concentrated his various forces in this region. Shaikh Nasr Al Madhkur sought help of the Shaikh of Grane (Kuwait) offering peace between them, but Grane refused it unless Shaikh Nasr agreed to pay half the revenues from Bahrain and a large proportion of revenues from Bushire. This indicated the confidence which both Grane and Zubara felt in their mutual alliance. It is possible that Shaikh Nasr intended to create a breach between the two allies by asking for peace from Grane so that he was free to attack Zubara.

Special situation

At the end of December 1782 Shaikh Nasr's expedition was on its way to Bahrain and forces were gathering on the Persian coast such as Janaba, Dashistan, Bandariq and Hormuz, and were patrolling the waters between Bahrain and the Qatar peninsula and imposing a naval blockade on Zubara as a show of strength. At the beginning of May 1783,[26] Shaikh Nasr Al Madhkur reached Bahrain so that he could personally oversee the operations.

In Zubara, the movements of Shaikh Nasr and the concentration of his forces had been observed by Nasr ever since the development of friction with him at the end of 1782. Shaikh Ahmed Bin Mohammed Al Khalifa mobilized his forces for the battle and took necessary defensive measures for confronting the blockade and the expected attack. He built up stocks of food, ammunition and water, so that he could face a long siege, if necessary. The desert route behind Zubara was open. He mobilized all able-bodied men capable of fighting and deployed them in the fort and along the fences. He placed women and children inside the fort, and appointed elderly people of the Al Khalifa to guard them. They were asked to kill these women and children if the Al Khalifa lost the battle so that they would not be captured. This showed the determination of the leaders to fight for victory or martyrdom.

During the blockade, Mir Ghani, the ruler of Bandariq, attempted to mediate between Shaikh Nasr and Shaikh Ahmed with a view to preventing bloodshed. Shaikh Nasr proposed extremely stiff terms for peace, and the mediation proved futile. Another mediation attempt followed by Shaikh Rashid al-Qasimi, the ruler of Julfar (Ras al-Khaimah), but this also was doomed to failure because of the obduracy and pride of Shaikh Nasr. Zubara was represented, during these negotiations, by Shaikh Abdulla Bin Khalifa Bin Ahmed Al Khalifa. The Al Khalifa agreed to return the booty which they had captured from Bahrain during their raid on it in September 1782, but Shaikh Nasr Al Madhkur demanded raid on it in September 1782, but Shaikh Nasr Al Madhkur demanded the unconditional surrender of the people of Zubara and the unfettered right to decide their fate. This made the Al Khalifa and the people of Zubara even more determined to fight; there was no alternative to facing the aggressors.

Shaikh Mohammed Bin Ahmed Al Khalifa took advantage of the long blockade and the period of negotiations to strengthen his defences and to increase his forces with the tribal supporters of Al Khalifa. His forces reached a high standard of readiness for battle whereas some of the forces of Shaikh Nasr were suffering the boredom of a long siege conducted far away from their homes.

Strategies

Shaikh Nasr planned to impose a naval blockade on Zubara and to strangle its trade until it submitted to his conditions. If this failed he would make a last-ditch attempt to storm the city.

However, the plan of Shaikh Ahmed Al Khalifa was to hold out against the blockade however long it lasted, and to launch a counter-attack against Shaikh Nasr's forces outside the town whenever an opportunity arose, in order to drive them off.

Course of the battle

When the blockade failed to subdue Zubara, the forces of Shaikh Nasr landed on 13 Jumadal al Akhira 1179 H/17 May 1783,[27] at a place between Zubara and Fureiha called Ashairaj on the north-west of Qatar Peninsula. From there they started their march towards Zubara. Skirmishes continued for a few days and by Friday, 22 Jumad Al Tania 1197 H/26 May 1783, the attackers were able to begin their siege of Zubara at prayer time. This time was chosen for its surprise element and because the people were engrossed in prayers at the mosques. As soon as the news of the landing of Shaikh Nasr's forces spread, people started rushing excitedly to join the battle. Those who had gathered for prayers at Fureiha rushed to the help of their brothers in Zubara. While the defenders of Zubara fought the attacking forces, the reinforcements coming from Fureiha arrived and a fierce battle ensued. Skirmishes had already occurred on the coast as soon as the forces had disembarked. The Utoob of Zubara and their supporters stood firm in their positions outside the perimeter of the city.

The battle gained in intensity but the attackers were unable to make any appreciable progress, and disaffection soon started sweeping through their ranks. The stage was now set for the final blow. Shaikh Ahmed Bin Mohammed Al Khalifa directed this in the form of a sweeping counter-attack by the forces which were positioned on the higher ground, reinforced by troops from Zubara and elsewhere. The reinforcements from Fureiha started attacking the invaders from the rear and turned their flanks. A fierce slaughter ensued and the attacking forces fled towards their ships, leaving their dead and wounded on the battlefield. Ultimately, Shaikh Nasr's entire force was defeated. Among those killed in the battle were Shaikh Mohammed, the nephew of Shaikh Nasr, and some other prominent men of Hormuz.

On the same day a naval force arrived from Grane consisting of six galliots and a number of boats as reinforcements. They attacked Bahrain where Shaikh Nasr's forces were forced to withdraw to the fort. The attacking force returned to Grane and within a few hours Shaikh Nasr received the news of the failure of his attack on Zubara. He decided to withdraw from the Arab coast immediately[28] and return to Bushire on 12 June 1783.

Lessons learnt

1 *Leadership and morale*

The leadership of Shaikh Ahmed Al Khalifa in Zubara was noted for its determination and resolution in facing a threat. The enemy demanded the total surrender of Zubara including women, children and servants under threat of death. They faced a severe test from these arrogant demands. Death meant nothing to them in the defence of their honour and their women and children. The people's determination was reflected in their soldiers who were totally steadfast in confronting the enemy. The support extended to them by the neighbouring tribes was also important in maintaining high morale among the defenders.

On the side of the attackers, the death of Mohammed, the nephew of Shaikh Nasr Al Madhkur, who was leader of the expedition, and of the nephew of Shaikh Rashid al-Qasimi, the ruler of Ras al Khaimah, as well as other leading figures of Hormuz who accompanied the expedition, led to the weakening of their morale. They were filled with foreboding. Word had passed round that Shaikh Nasr had taken part in the battle but his sword had fallen into the hands of Salama Al Bin Ali and he had fled to Bushire. This showed the degree of demoralization among the ranks of the leaders and troops of the attacking force.

2 Defensive measures

Shaikh Ahmed Al Khalifa made preparations for the battle of Zubara. He was ready for a prolonged struggle because he had adopted the necessary measures for defence and the procurement of supplies. The result of the battle showed that he had an excellent strategy in the deployment of his troops and assigning them to vital positions. He had a good appreciation of the proper time for launching a counter-attack. In this case the defence deflected the aggression because of good planning. It was a positive and offensive defence and not a passive one.

Offensive action is an important principle of defence. It means that the side which takes up a defensive posture because of the strength of the enemy should be offensive in spirit and strike at the enemy from time to time to wear him down by firing on his positions, raiding them and sending out fighting patrols. Finally, a counter-blow should be delivered when the opportunity presents itself.

3 Information

The information about the concentration of the expeditionary forces of Nasr Al Madhkur and their advance towards Zubara reached Shaikh Ahmed Al Khalifa well before the arrival of the force itself. This gave him sufficient time to adopt counter-measures to confront the invaders. There is no doubt that this depended on a system of obtaining intelligence by directly observing and closely following the enemy's movements. The invading forces failed to camouflage their movement, or practise any methods of deception. This may have been because of Shaikh Nasr and his nephew's arrogant confidence in their own strength.

4 Co-operation and initiative

Co-operation between the people of Zubara and the surrounding areas enabled them to combine closely in the face of the coming danger. The reinforcements sent by the people of Fureiha and their landing in the rear of the enemy in an encircling movement was an important factor in sowing confusion in the ranks of the striking forces. It provided an opportunity to pin down the enemy and prepare the way for the launching of a counter-attack by the people of Zubara. As soon as the attacking forces landed on the coast they were harassed by the defenders positioned on the various small hills around Zubara and by the advancing reinforcements. In this way the Utoob of Zubara and their supporters regained the initiative. Thus one can impose one's will on the enemy. The leaders of the attacking force, on the other hand, were doubtful and hesitant and they concentrated all their hopes on prolonging the siege to achieve their aim.

5 Offensive spirit

War and politics are the two means of achieving the same end. These are the twin means of struggle available to every statesman and warrior. It appears that the will to fight among the people of Zubara was stronger than that of their adversaries both for the political leadership and for the soldiers. They were inspired to fight to protect their honour and dignity while the attackers were drawn by the lure of plunder and booty. The will to fight is strengthened by the presence of competent leaders, faith in a cause, morale and training. The Arabian Peninsula has always produced examples of great warriors ever since the beginning of the seventh century AD. The fighting spirit and the love of heroism are deep-rooted among the people of the Arabian Peninsula even since before the advent of Islam. They take their greatest pride in courage and audacity. When they were united by the Islamic faith, their will was reinforced with moral and spiritual strength and they became a mighty force which nothing could withstand.

6 Deception and surprise

Deception was used to mislead the invaders about the arrival of reinforcements at Zubara. This was achieved by showing the camels carrying imaginary loads and making feinting movements. The timing of the attack of the people of Fureiha and the counter-attack succeeded in surprising the attackers who lost their balance both physically and morally. It struck terror in their ranks and unbalanced their leadership, thus causing their defeat.

7 Administrative measures

The Utoob of Zubara took various administrative measures to resist a long siege. It was easy for them to supply their troops with food and water since they were on their own soil and their lines of communication were short. The enemy's supply bases were either in Bushire hundred of miles across the sea or scores of miles away in Bahrain. These over-extended lines of communication required much effort for the attacking forces to secure particularly when the siege was prolonged without any decisive results. This was a factor which affected the determination and fighting spirit of the invaders.

8 A fighting population

The population of Zubara was converted into fighting soldiers. Thus the principle of concentration of force was being exploited. This force had specific and clear-cut objectives. The aim was either victory or martyrdom in defence of the motherland. They were clear about the calamity which would befall their women and children if they hesitated

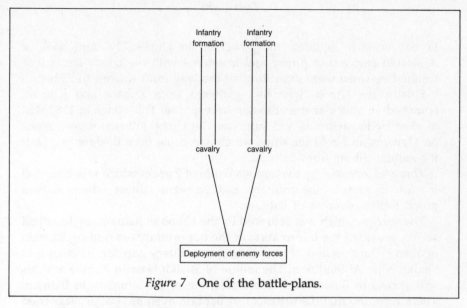

Figure 7 One of the battle-plans.

to confront the enemy. They therefore showed great patience and endurance. They were not frightened by the numbers of the enemy. They won a collective victory as a fighting people who were closely united in the face of danger.

D The Battle of Bahrain

General situation

The ruler of Bahrain was an Arab who used to pay tribute to Persia when its influence was in the ascendant. Meanwhile the political and merchant communities in Zubara were progressing during the time of the Al Khalifa and their supporters among the Arab tribes. Bahrain was inhabited by some of the Utoob and their supporters such as the Al Fadhil and others. When the power of the Utoob expanded along the western coast of the Gulf from Kuwait to Qatar and their ports gained prosperity, especially Zubara and Kuwait, the Arab shaikhs of the eastern coast moved against them as they regarded them as competitors. They confronted their ships and the rivalry between them became fierce. Because of the weakening of Persian influence on the eastern coast of the Gulf, the Arabs there enjoyed relative freedom from Persian interference. In 1777 the ruler of Bushire tried to attack Zubara just as the Bani Kaab had also attacked the Utoob ships in Zubara and Kuwait, and Ali Murad Khan in Isfahan goaded the shaikhs of the eastern

Persian coast to liquidate the power of the Utoob. The Bani Kaab of Arabistan engaged in piracy and interfered with the Utoob and a war resulted between them extending all the way from Kuwait to Zubara.

Finally, the Utoob, who had gathered from Zubara and Kuwait, launched an attack against Bahrain in response. This attack in 1782 was marked by its swiftness and surprise. The Utoob inflicted severe losses on Manama and held the ships which had come from Bushire to collect the annual tribute from Bahrain.

This was followed by the famous Battle of Zubara which was intended to put an end to the military and economic threat which Zubara posed to the governor of Bahrain.

The success which was achieved by the Utoob in Bahrain, as described above, provided the information of the opportunity for ridding Bahrain of alien influences and of overcoming its military garrison belonging to Shaikh Nasr Al Madhkur. The failure of Shaikh Nasr in Zubara and his withdrawal to Bushire led to a worsening of the situation in Bahrain. There were internal disturbances in Bahrain even as Shaikh Nasr tried to mount another expedition against Zubara with the participation of some shaikhdoms along the coast. However, the attempt failed and further weakened the position of Shaikh Nasr in Bahrain. The news of sedition and disturbances in Bahrain reached Shaikh Ahmed Bin Mohammed Al Khalifa and encouraged him to launch a decisive move for its liberation. Bahrain was ready to accept someone who would free it from all foreign influences.

Special situation

During the few weeks that followed the Battle of Zubara, repeated news of insecurity and disturbances in Bahrain reached Shaikh Ahmed Bin Mohammed Al Khalifa. There were reports of internal dissension among its people, some of whom were said to be supporting the Utoob. He saw that the opportunity had arrived for decisive action in Bahrain. He started urgent preparations to gather the necessary forces. Shaikh Nasr, on the other hand, failed in all his attempts of mobilize the forces with which he could regain his influence in the Gulf after the Battle of Zubara. Information soon arrived that he did not have sufficient force to protect the island or recover it with foreign assistance. Persia was facing a civil war between the members of the ruling family at that time.

Progress of the battle

Shaikh Ahmed completed the mobilization of his forces and advanced towards Bahrain in the month of Shaban 1197 H or mid-July 1783. As soon as his forces disembarked, the garrison of Bahrain and the family of Shaikh Nasr and his supporters sought shelter in the Dewan Fort of Manama and the Bahrain Fort of Jaboor. Shaikh Ahmed's forces closed in on the two fortresses and besieged them. (It has proved impossible to discover any contemporary documents, including British documents, which could throw light on the strength of the Bahrain garrison or the number of ships which were used by Shaikh Ahmed to land his troops in Bahrain.) After the blockading of the two forts the process of storming them took place in two phases.

Phase I

Storming of the Dewan Fort (this is the fort which is today occupied by the Interior Ministry). The fort was speedily stormed from an unexpected direction, achieving surprise. There was a spring inside the fort from which water flowed northwards outside the fort. This was covered with a roof-like a tunnel with several ventilators. The canal went into an orchard in Manama and the people in the adjacent houses made use of its water. Shaikh Ahmed selected a group of strong fighters to form a special force with the task of entering the fort through the tunnel.

These men at once entered the canal at its opening and made for the small gate of the fort. They opened the small gate while the forces which were ready outside rushed to enter the fort. They overwhelmed the garrison which quickly laid down their arms and surrendered. There were some women and children from the family of Shaikh Nasr in the fort. Shaikh Ahmed Al Khalifa gave orders for them to be transported by ship to Bushire, and asked Ali Bin Khalifa Al Fadhil to escort them in safety to their families. This was done. When the family of Shaikh Nasr Al Madkhur and their followers were returned to their relatives in Bushire with all respect and consideration, Shaikh Nasr praised this as a noble action. It made a great impact on the enemies of Shaikh Ahmed Al Khalifa who lauded this truly noble and chivalrous Arab-Islamic spirit.

Phase II

The remainder of Shaikh Nasr's men in the Bahrain garrison remained inside the Bahrain fort of Jaboor, Shaikh Ahmed Al Khalifa surrounded it and ordered its blockade. In their hopeless situation, the garrison surrendered on Wednesday 22 Shaban 1197 H/23 July 1783.[29] Shaikh Ahmed Bin Mohammed Al Khalifa distributed the booty among his soldiers of the Arab tribes who had participated in the battle. He appointed a man named Ajaj as the commander of the fort which came to be known as the Ajaj Fort. This Ajaj was the ancestor of the Ajaj family of Muharraq today. Finally, Shaikh Ahmed converted this fort into a prison.

By virtue of this swift and courageous attack on Bahrain, Shaikh Ahmed Bin Mohammed Al Khalifa earned the title of Al-Fateh, 'the Conqueror'. The date of his victory is recorded as 1197 H/AD 1783.[30]

It was thus that Bahrain returned to Arab rule.

Shaikh Ahmed organized the affairs of state, established his authority and created a normal situation before returning to Zubara. He appointed a ruler over Bahrain as his representative. This was Shaikh Ali Bin Faris, who was a poet and scholar. Ibn Sanad says in this context: 'The ruler of Awal, Shaikh Ahmed Bin Mohammed Al Khalifa, appointed Shaikh Ali Bin Faris as a governor who adorned the post with his lofty character and mature opinions. He established his headquarters in the Dewan fort located near Manama.' Shaikh Ahmed used to spend his summers in Bahrain and winters in Zubara. With the advent of spring, Shaikh Ahmed used to frequent a rectangular garden area in Aali in Bahrain. When the rainy season arrived, it used to turn green with a spring gushing out of it. Once the situation in Bahrain had stabilized, the country started to progress economically in an atmosphere of peace and security. Trade flourished between India and the northern Gulf passing through Zubara and Bahrain in particular. The disturbed conditions prevailing in Persia and its coastal areas also helped to promote the prosperity of Bahrain and Zubara. At the same time it aroused jealousy and greed among the neighbouring foreign powers.

Bahrain and Zubara faced many incidents engineered by the ambitious adjoining states in the beginning of the twelfth century of Hijra. Zubara therefore prepared to defend itself. Shaikh Ahmed al-Fateh rallied the people of Zubara and Bahrain and held consultations with them about the best way of defending the country. The necessary steps were taken in this regard. One of these was to dig a trench extending from the sea to the Marir Fort in Zubara in the form of a canal. Shaikh Ahmed advised his people to build fortifications and towers on both sides of the channel which could protect the ships right

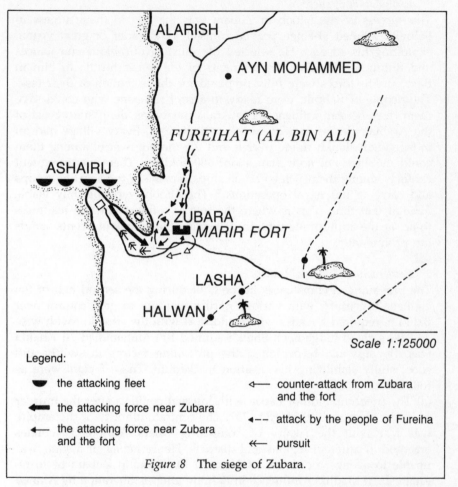

Figure 8 The siege of Zubara.

up to the fort. The residents of Zubara and Bahrain affirmed before Ahmed al-Fateh that they would bear the expenses of digging it. In due course an integrated defence plan was put into operation. Shaikh Ahmed al-Fateh finally died in 1209 H/AD 1795.[31]

Lessons learnt

After a study of the conditions which prevailed in the Gulf region and an analysis of various attitudes which were adopted both before and after the Battle of Zubara, it is possible to discern the various factors which contributed to certain victory. The following lessons stand out:

1 Exploitation of success

The success of the Utoob in Zubara was the key to their success in Bahrain. Ahmed al-Fateh proved himself as a leader of great vision, exploiting his success. He selected the most favourable circumstances and timing to liquidate the remnants of the forces hostile to him in Bahrain. His forces were fully prepared for the execution of their task. The people of Bahrain were ready to accept someone who could save them from Persian influence. The Arabs inhabiting the eastern coast of the Arabian Peninsula were weak and divided. Every village had an independent shaikh ruling over it and the more powerful among them could mobilize no more than about 400 soldiers. There were frequent conflicts among them. They had no ships capable of transporting troops and carrying out naval operations.[32] The Utoob were the only viable force at that time. This is where the role of a force with the readiness to act at the appropriate time to determine the course of events stands out prominently.

2 Leadership and far-sightedness

The prevailing circumstances in the Gulf during the second half of the eighteenth century, with various parties wanting to gain control over Bahrain, required a leader who could deal with the situation with wise and far-sighted judgement. Shaikh Ahmed Bin Mohammed Al Khalifa was the answer. He exploited the prevailing factors in swiftly and successfully stabilizing his position in Bahrain. These factors were as follows:

(a) The preoccupation of Persia with internal conflicts after the murder of Nadir Shah in 1160 H/AD 1747. The central authority of the empire was lost with the rivalry of competing rulers. Various potentates emerged in different regions and districts. Hence Persia, as a state, was unable to avenge the defeat of Nasr Al Madhkur in Zubara or to re-establish Al Madhkur influence in Bahrain after its liberation by Ahmed al-Fateh.[33]

(b) The naval weakness of the Ottomans in the Gulf region during that period did not permit them to move sufficient ground troops to the theatre of operations. Their authority had not yet spread over the various parts of the region. The Ottomans were preoccupied with their wars in Europe and elsewhere.[34]

3 Speed and surprise

The speedy move of Ahmed al-Fateh towards Bahrain was an important factor in achieving surprise over its garrison as well as others who coveted Bahrain. These parties did not have sufficient time to react in a decisive and co-ordinated fashion. Thus events turned against them.

For instance, Dutch reports from Kharaj[35] referred to British interest in gaining control over Bahrain, and Savage, the director of the East India Company in Gombroon (Bandar Abbas), had prepared a plan for the conquest of Bahrain. A few months previously he had been in London, and before that two British ships had been frequenting Bahrain to prepare a map of the country. British espionage activities increased, and a report stated that a British merchant named Dodd, who was with Savage in Gombroon, had paid several visits to Bushire, Bandariq and Gombroon over a period of six months. There were indications that the British were preparing something when they ordered two ships to be built in Bombay. This caused the Dutch to conclude that the British wanted to occupy Bahrain.

The operations launched by Ahmed al-Fateh forestalled their plans. The use of speed and surprise enabled a leader of his kind to turn the tables on the enemy and succeed against the odds.

4 Offensive action and initiative

Ahmed al-Fateh continued throughout to hold to the principles of offensive action and initiative while moving his troops to Bahrain, storming the Dewan Fort and continuing his strikes against the forces which were besieged within the Bahrain Fort until they surrendered. In seizing the initiative, he was able to impose his will on the enemy and make him react in a way which had already taken into account. It was something new for his opponent.

5 Intelligence

After his defeat in Zubara and his return to the Persian coast, Shaikh Nasr Al Madhkur sent a letter to the Commander of the Bahrain garrison asking him to hold out until reinforcements reached him. The ship which was carrying this letter was captured. It showed the situation Shaikh Nasr's forces were in and it was of great importance to Shaikh Ahmed al-Fateh to know their condition and state of morale. There is no doubt that he gathered intelligence from other sources which helped him to seize the opportunity to deliver the blow at the right time and place.

6 Morale

As a result of their ignominious defeat and heavy losses in Zubara the forces of Shaikh Nasr and his allies were confused and of extremely low morale. Their defeatism affected those who were left in Bahrain. They felt helpless as they had only two ships left from the remnants of the fleet of Nadir Shah, and even these were not sea-worthy.[36] The allegiance to Persia of Shaikh Jabara and the Al Madhkur who were in charge of the affairs of Bahrain was weak. When Shaikh Jabara went to perform the Haj pilgrimage, his authority was usurped by Shaikh Nasr Al Madhkur. The lack of firm loyalty among the leaders indicated low morale. On the other hand, the morale of the forces of Shaikh Ahmed al-Fateh was high because of their success and their superb leadership. Success begets success. The operations in Bahrain were a further blow to Shaikh Nasr Al Madhkur when his forces were already reeling under the defeat they had just suffered at Zubara.

7   Value of fortifications in defence

The Bahrain garrison retreated into their fortresses when the forces of Ahmed al-Fateh landed on the coast. This showed a trench mentality seeking self-protection, and not a fighting or offensive spirit. It also showed the reality of the value of fortifications in defensive operations. Fortifications can enable forces to hold out and defend themselves for a certain period by holding up the enemy and keeping a part of his forces engaged until reinforcements arrive but they cannot hold out for long in the face of a determined enemy imbued with an offensive spirit. Fortresses cannot help for long if their occupants do not show an offensive spirit by engaging the enemy and winning a decisive battle. Military history is full of examples which drive home this lesson, such as the Maginot, Siegfried and Bar-Lev Lines. All these defensive lines were stormed by trained attacking forces within a short time.

Date of Battles of Zubara and Bahrain

After a long siege the forces of Nasr Al Madhkur landed on Zubara on 13 Jumad al Akhira 1197 H/17 May 1783. A decisive battle followed in Zubara on 18 Jamad al Akhira/May 22, in which Nasr was defeated before he fled to Bushire.

Document reference: IOR R/15/1/3 of 26 June 1783 and Nabhani p. 125. Shaikh Nasr reached Bushire after his defeat in the Battle of Zubara on 10 Rajan 1197/12 June 1783.

IOR 15/1/3 to 194 of 26 June 1783 and Nabhini p. 125. The garrison of Bahrain under the leadership of Shaikh Rashid, the nephew of Shaikh Nasr Al Madhkur, surrendered on Wednesday, 22 Shaban 1197 H/23 July 1783.

Shaikh Rashid, the nephew of Shaikh Nasr, reached Bushire on 6th Ramadan 1197 H/5 August 1783 from Bahrain after his surrender.

Lessons learnt from battles of confrontation

Bahrain enjoyed a spell of peace and stability after its liberation by Shaikh Ahmed al-Fateh and the people of Bahrain welcomed the new administration. Nevertheless, it attracted the attention of greedy neighbouring powers wanting to establish control over it in view of the importance of its location, abundance water resources and wealth derived especially from its pearl-banks. Anyone who studies the history of the campaigns in Bahrain from the beginning of the thirteenth century Hijra/nineteenth century AD can understand how it confronted the greed of the foreign forces through sound military planning and wise leadership, exploiting the principles of offensive action and initiative. Sound and rapid preparations for a well equipped force capable of striking at the enemy before he could complete his own preparations threw him into confusion and secured victory. An attack on the enemy in his own bases, means you are choosing the time and place of battle and imposing your will upon him. The reaction of the enemy can be anticipated by the attackers.

Speed and surprise can be achieved by moving ships at night to reach their objective suddenly and unexpectedly. Another element of surprise was the size of the forces deployed which struck terror in the hearts of the enemy who tried to avoid an unequal battle. These produced the first signs of psychological weakening in the enemy command. The swiftness of movement during deployment and the conduct of battle at the chosen place both contributed to victory.

The nature of the terrain helped in achieving victory because the places where the fighting took place were mostly covered with date-palm and the coastline was marshy. At low tide the enemy ships had to anchor far away from their forces. The field of operations, dominated by the plentiful date-palms, is the same for all combatants. However, in most battles the Bahraini forces had defenders on the coast to drive back the enemy into the sea. The army was split into several groups of infantry in the centre together with the command headquarters. There was also a division of cavalry on the right and another on the left. When the opposing forces closed in, the two cavalry divisions made a rapid encircling movement against the enemy while the infantry in the centre launched a direct attack from the front. Compared with the tactics of the Bahraini forces those of the enemy's commanders were circumscribed by the nature of the terrain and the need to stay close to the ships which acted as their base. Moreover, the enemy forces attacking Bahrain did not have any cavalry, which provided the speed and decisive action in battle. On the other hand, the Bahraini tactics were both offensive in character and flexible in adapting to changes in the situation. The Bahraini's cavalry had at their disposal strategic depth of territory and a secure base for their forces.[37]

The lessons learnt from the study of the history of various battles in Bahrain of the nineteenth century, show that every battle had one or more special factors which contributed to success. In some of the battles the enemy had static defences in a specific location on the coast close to their ships. This was a drawback for the enemy because it allowed the Bahraini command freedom to concentrate and move their forces, to take all necessary measures in their rear possible and choose the time of attack. Had the enemy attacked the main targets immediately after landing and maintained their offensive momentum, the results would have been different.

While simplicity and flexibility are the ideal of any military strategy, the enemy plans in Bahrain were dictated by the shape of the terrain. The enemy did not take into consideration the tactical advantages of the Bahraini leadership, or consider ways of countering them. They did not take the various possibilities into account. The Bahraini leadership, on the other hand, took all possible factors into consideration and catered for all eventualities. Hence their tactics were very flexible, bold and practical. They proved superior to the rigid and static strategy of their opponents. Outflanking moves from one or more directions are one of the best means of achieving speedy and decisive results.

Military history provides numerous examples of the success of such a strategy. In the battle of Cannae in 216 BC in which Hannibal defeated the Roman armies, it was his double enflanking movement carried out by two divisions of cavalry which destroyed the superior Roman army. The battle has remained as a great lesson in military history which is likely to stand the test of time. The German military leadership, at the beginning of this century, laid great emphasis on the training of their officers on this type of operation wherever the circumstances occurred.

The manoeuvres of the Bahraini cavalry in their enveloping movement against the enemy are a fine example of leadership. It achieved decisive results in a short time and with minimal losses. The availability of the cavalry, which the enemy lacked, made it simpler. The Bahraini forces benefited from the use of camouflage and deception by hiding their forces for a long time in date-palm groves until the enemy believed that their forces were few in number. It showed the weakness of enemy intelligence. He did not know of various measures which were being taken on the Bahraini side. All these measures combined to cause surprise and sow confusion in enemy ranks.

References

1   J. G. Lorimer, *The Gazetteer of the Gulf*, Historical Section, vol. 3, p. 1270, Calcutta, 1915. Karkani says on p. 153 that Shaikh Madhkur was of the tribe of Bu Mahair. Similarly, see Abbas Faroqi, p. 68, and *Al Watheeka*, No. 2, p. 93.

2   Shaibani, Mohammed Sharif, *The History of the Arab Tribes on the Persian Coasts*, pp. 140–1, Beirut, 1968.

3   Lorimer, *The Gazetteer of the Gulf*, Historical Section, vol. 3, p. 1270. Karim Khan ruled from 1163 to 1193 H and was the first Zand ruler of Persia. See *The History of Iran*, by Mohammed Hajazi (in Persian), pp. 202–9, Iran, 1346 H.

4   *Al Watheeka*, No. 11, p. 120, note 78.

5   J. G. Lorimer, *The Gazetteer of the Gulf*, Historical Section, vol. 3, p. 1273, Calcutta, 1915.

6   Quoted by Shaikh Ibrahim Bin Mohammed Al Khalifa.

7   Francis Warden *A Historical Sketch of the Arab Tribe of Utoob.*

8   Al Bassa. The *ulemas* (scholars) of Nejd, 1/229, 230. The verse mentioned by Shaikh Mohammed Bin Isa Bin Ali Al Khalifa is quoted by Dr Abu Hakima in the marginal notes of his discourse on p. 93, cited in Abu Hakima, *The History of Kuwait*, p. 105.

9   A Dutch document from the Archives of Holland. It was published in *Al Watheeka*, No. 3, in the course of a report written by Kniphausen, Director of the Dutch East India Company in Kharag in 1168 H/AD 1754, and was translated into English by Dr Slot. See the Ottoman Document No. D M 111, p. 713 which states: 'The Utoob had guns and their ships were equipped with guns too.' This is contrary to what is contained in the Dutch document. See the report of J. H. Lovett of 28 November 1798, pp. 323–4. (G29/25).

10 Shaikh Khalifa Bin Mohammed Al Khalifa. His maternal uncles were Al Sabah. His uncle was Shaikh Sabah Bin Jaber. This Khalifa had a son by the name of Abdulla whose progeny still survives. See notes in *Tohfat al Nab'haniyya*, p. 128. The maternal uncles of Shaikh Muqrin Bin Mohammed Bin Khalifa were from Al Bin Ali as stated earlier. This Muqrin had a son Mohammed who was imprisoned in Muscat in Jalali Fort.

    The maternal uncles of Shaikh Ibrahim Bin Mohammed Bin Khalifa and his brother Shaikh Ali hailed from Al Bukawara from Al Shaikh. See notes in *Tohfat al Nab'haniyya*, p. 128.

11 Tabatabai, Abdul Jaleeli Yassin, Ruwad al Khall Wal Khalil, *The Poetical Works of Sayyed Abdul Jeleel* (Preface and 'Sabayik al Asjad' by Shaikh Ibn Sanad), pp. 19–20.

12 Mirza Hassan Khan, *The History of the Governorate of Basra*, p. 122, published by the Centre of Gulf Studies at the Basra University, 1980. Ibn Sanad Othaman, *Matali Al Saud bin Teeb Akhbar Al Wali Dawood*, pp. 3–4, printed in Bombay in 1304 H.

13 Ibn Bashair, *Unwan Al Majd fi Tareekh Nejd*, 1/76. J. G. Lorimer, *The Gazetteer*

of the Gulf, Historical Section, vol. 3, p. 1196, Calcutta, 1915. Hydari Unwan al Majd (manuscript), pp. 87–8.

14 Ibn Sanad, *Sabayik Al Asjad*, p. 18.
15 Magazine *Al Arabi*, No. 248.
16 Khan, *History of Governorate of Basra*, p. 118; J. G. Lorimer, *The Gazetteer of the Gulf*, Historical Section, vol. 4, p. 1839–40, Calcutta, 1915, and al Azawi, vol. 6, p. 13, *Tohfat al Alam*.
17 Ibn Isa, *The History of Some of the Events of Nejd* (Arabic), pp. 111, 114, 115, 118 and 133. Ibn Sanad, *Sabayik Al Asjad*, pp. 23–103, and Abdul Rahman Al Shaikh, *Some Famous Scholars of Najd*, p. 188.
18 *Ibid.*, pp. 95, 119 and 121, and *History of Nejd*, vol. 2, pp. 76–7, Egypt, 1949.
19 A report by Jones about trade in Arab and Persian countries in 1205 H/ AD 1790. See Abu Hakima, *The History of Kuwait*, vol. 1, p. 20.
20 J. G. Lorimer, *The Gazetteer of the Gulf*, vol. 1, p. 787, Calcutta, 1915, and Abu Hakima, *The History of Kuwait*, p. 84.
21 A report by Latouche, the commercial resident in Basra, GG, 29/21, vol. xvii Despatch No. 1230.
22 Latouche: G 29/30, vol. xvii/1230, and Lorimer, vol. 2, p. 1197, and Belgrave, p. 6.
23 G 29/21 No. 1230/474, 4 November, 1782. Residency of Basra.
24 IOR R 15/1/3, No. 22 of 28 February 1783, pp. 187–8.
25 *Tohfat al Nab'haniyya*, pp. 123–4.
26 R 15/1/3 pp. 177–8, No. 7 of 30 March, 1782. The name has appeared as Nasr in Nab'hani, pp. 114–15, 2nd edition. The IOR documents refer to him as Nassir, perhaps because it is similar to pronounce. Persian sources, however, refer to him as Nasr Al Madhkur.
27 R 15/1/3, No. 26 of June 1783, p. 191.
28 IOR R 15/1/3, No. 26, June 1783.
29 *Ibid.*, No. 30 of 21 August, 1783.
30 Nabhani, pp. 126–7.
31 Lama'al Shihab, pp. 185–199 (manuscript).
32 Dutch document, vol. 2848, *Al Watheeka*, No. 11 of July 1987.
33 Dutch Archives, Floor, *Persica*, 8, 1979, p. 166; and Slot, a paper on the Dutch East India Company in the Gulf region between 1645 and 1765.
34 Dutch Document, Floor, *Persica*, 1979, pp. 178–9.
35 V O C 2864, pp. 5–6, Report by the Dutch residents, dated 8 January, 1756.
36 Floor, *Persica*, 1979, p. 166.
37 Nabhani, pp. 141–9.

CHAPTER 3

Independence

A Building an Independent State

At the end of 1961 the whole of Bahrain was brilliantly illuminated. All parts of the country were splendidly decorated and there were many happy celebrations on a grand scale. The people of Bahrain came out on to the streets in thousands to express their joy as they greeted their young Amir, Shaikh Isa Bin Salman Al Khalifa, who was taking over the rule of the country in the tradition of his forefathers as the leader of his people and the country. The Amir in his youthful vigour represented the aspirations of this young nation. The enthusiastic greetings of the people were a true reflection of their love for their Amir in whom they saw a wise leader capable of achieving for his country all its hopes of progress and development.

These gentle and noble people, among whom youth represents 70 per cent of the population, found in their young Amir a true reflection of their own aspirations. They felt that they had come close to realizing their ideals, and hence were expressing their feelings in the most genuine way that a people can show their leader.

The explosion of emotion for their leader which took hold of them in those days and in the following decades made them rally round him and show him their love and confidence which is the essential basis of the stability and security of a country during its first phase of an independent state and the overcoming of the various obstacles in its path. Later it became the basis of the great role which Bahrain played out of proportion to its size and potential. This could not have been done without the people's adherence to their cultural values as they rallied round their leader whom they trusted and loved. It was this wise and able leadership which was to lead the country towards prosperity and true independence.

The following facts and figures indicate the characteristics of this long and difficult task of building an independent state in the course of the last two decades. Before this it is worth not so much recounting and analysing historical events as briefly stating the basic issues involved and the priorities which were allotted to them at that time.

It was obvious from the very beginning of the succession of His Highness the Amir that the country was on the threshold of the era of independence. Therefore it was necessary to prepare psychologically and administratively for the momentous day. This preliminary period was characterized by the establishment of various state organs and institutions and a study of the national economy. His Highness Shaikh Khalifa Bin Salman Al Khalifa undertook to organize these affairs as the head of the central administration. Accordingly various studies were completed, the necessary expertise was brought in and various specialist offices were established to identify and classify the sources of income. The Monetary Agency was modernized and similarly specialized directorates of information and foreign affairs were established. Public services were placed under different departments (which later on became the nuclei for the various ministries which were formed after independence). The administration of justice gradually developed from primary courts to the creation of a judiciary independent from the executive. The first decade had not ended when in about 1968 the various administrative organs of state and economic policy were prepared to play an active role in the period ahead.

During the period, His Highness the Amir devoted much attention towards strengthening his relations with his brother presidents and heads of state and governments in the area. He made a series of visits to the Gulf States where His Highness made the most sincere and extensive efforts to solve the legal and political problems with neighbouring States. In the year 1970 Bahrain was faced with two alternatives. One was to join a union of the brother states in the region so that each state would have enough time to build a sound basic infrastructure for a federal state in the future.

When it became clear that this path had been chosen, Bahrain realized that its national duty was to build up a security and defence potential. Therefore certain basic developments were introduced into the internal security forces and a basis was laid for reorganizing the Directorate of Police as an integrated Ministry of the Interior. I was entrusted with the task of raising a defence force in the country. Hence the National Guard was formed to act as a nucleus for the Bahrain Defence Force which came into existence soon after the achievement of independence.

After a difficult period of preparation and discussion, Bahrain announced its independence in 1971 (which was the tenth anniversary of His Highness the Amir's accession as ruler). The big popular celebrations held to herald the event showed the extent of public support for His Highness Shaikh Isa Bin Salman Al Khalifa as the Amir of a free country as the people of Bahrain demonstrated their wish to remain an independent Arab state and masters of their own destiny now and in the future.

The era of independence had several characteristic features which are difficult to separate historically because they come to the fore at different periods and are intermingled with each other. It is not easy to isolate one from the other in terms of time. However, I shall restrict myself to mentioning a few important points.

First, Bahrain entered a period of having to adopt a participatory political system. It laid down a constitution, which was ratified by the National Council, based on the principles of selection and appointment. Later, Bahrain undertook a parliamentary experiment and gained experience from it. It will benefit from it in its political organization based on participation and consultation and I hope that we shall be able to realize it within the framework of the experiment in unification of the Gulf Co-operation Council or something similar.

Secondly, the recent past has been characterized by a unique kind of economic prosperity as Bahrain became a great centre for oil and financial services, air services, communications as well as for the oil, aluminium and ship-building industries and for ship-repairing.

Thirdly, Bahrain in its powerful thrust towards economic activity has not neglected the social and humanitarian aspects of life which are normally made more significant by economic progress. So Bahrain constructed new townships and residential complexes, organized the health services and provided employment opportunities for all its citizens. Thus it ensured for its people a life of dignity and plenty. Bahrain also took care of the aged and the handicapped among its population and provided them with all possible assistance.

Fourthly, on the basis of the popular saying 'A sound mind in a sound body', Bahrain devoted a great deal of attention to youth and constantly endeavoured to promote sports in the country. It patronized clubs and participated in various tournaments and sports competitions at the regional, Arab and international levels. Thus the standard of sports was raised along with the people's aspirations. A sense of national pride took firm root in the minds of the youth of the country.

Fifthly, the country paid strong and fundamental attention to the development of education in its various stages. After sixty years of the existence of schools at primary, preparatory and secondary levels, Bahrain started thinking of providing higher education for its people to enable them, through the instillation of sound and scientific thinking, to achieve their aspirations. It gave them the choice of selecting scientific and vocational studies which would assure them and their country prosperity and progress. Bahrain today boasts of three institutions of higher education after three decades of the rule of His Highness the Amir.

The 1980s gave Bahrain hope and confidence and encouraged it towards greater regional cooperation with the other states of the Gulf who are bound together by the regional organization, the Gulf Co-operation Council, which aims at fusing the potentials of the region in a single crucible for the achievement of economic integration leading ultimately if God wills, to unification. The Bahraini people who have followed their youthful leader for three decades continue on their march towards a bright future with firm and confident steps. Thanks to the excellent rapport between the leader and his people, they are satisfied with his wise leadership as he constantly works to achieve greater prosperity, and progress for the present and future generations of Bahrain.

B Preparations for General Military Service

From ancient times to the present the environment has been a formative element in man's development. I used on various occasions to listen to the narration of stories concerned with our history. These sessions were like school lessons where the teacher concentrated on our heroes and their exploits. I used to listen avidly as the history of the various wars, the conduct of great leaders, the campaigns they waged, the factors which contributed to victory or defeat, were narrated. How I wished at that time that we should, as a nation, study the reasons for our defeats as well as our successes so that we could learn the lessons and benefit from them. History often repeats itself and different battles resemble one another in several ways. The differences are minor, especially where the forces are restricted to a specific area or region. An example of this is Palestine where the enemy, for a long time and even up to the present, has used the same strategy in all battles even if his mobilization training, the extent and types of his firepower and his manoeuvres have differed to some extent.

The stories revealed our nation's glorious history since the dawn of Islam, and the noble values it stood for which filled an Arab and Muslim with pride and confidence in contrast to an opponent who is unscrupulous, degrades humanity and only scores certain temporary successes in battles against our nation in modern times. In the course of various sessions I and my colleagues heard the history of our forefathers and of their courage and chivalry and I used to be happy with the determination and courage shown by our people even if, on occasions, we heard the news over the radio and from visiting delegations about events in our nation, the setbacks it suffered, its lagging behind in the march of civilization, and in the creation of the basic framework of a deterrent military power. This put us in a quandary over the question of regaining our usurped rights and the painful realities of life faced by our Arab nation. We are an indivisible part of it. It is an outstanding nation imbued with the glory of Islam.

There is, therefore, a problem with makes heavy demands. It is up to us to deal with it sincerely and practically, and not merely with words. We should establish our priorities and define the goals of joint action to make full use of our potential. With this aim in mind, we started preparing ourselves on the basis of sound thinking to protect our noble heritage with full faith in mutual endeavour. This was our response to the painful setback suffered by our Arab nation. We started our move forwards with firm and well-considered steps and with hope and confidence in a better future with God's help.

I studied the Holy Quran and reflected on it. It refers in several places to the need for holy struggle. I became convinced that struggle in the cause of God and the country was a sacred duty because the conduct and character of the Holy Prophet provides a great example of faith and struggle until victory over falsehood had been achieved. It became apparent from a study of our history, including the history of various Islamic conquests and resistance against invaders and colonizers, that we were cast in the mould of struggle from the outset. Periods of mourning, the offering of prayers for the souls of our martyrs, the Algerian fight for independence and the struggle of the Palestinian people, are all matters which stand out in my memory as though they happened only yesterday.

This was the type of society in which I lived. It was a great school of life in which I learnt a great deal in addition to what I had studied at school. All these prepared me to face the future and made me realize the responsibility towards Bahrain and its youth which had been cast upon my shoulders as Crown Prince. I therefore took the initiative to join one of the military colleges to enable me to study the science of modern warfare. I felt the need to absorb it in order to serve with all my potential the country which has given us so much in life. Soldiering was my means of serving this goal.

C First Steps

Bahrain always had a military capacity in the past. Its history bears witness to its ancient links with military matters. It recounts the battles and wars fought by Bahraini fleets over the ages although this is not the place for detailed narratives. Bahrain possessed one of the strongest naval fleets in the region over a long period. Even though the fleet was not manned with any regular forces during that time, it distinguished itself by the effectiveness in ensuring the protection of the country and confronting the enemies who coveted it. Thereafter, Bahrain went through a period in which it had to depend on foreign forces as a result of the prevailing international situation. Fortunately, this situation did not last long, as international circumstances changed. Thanks to the progress and enlightenment of our great Bahraini people and their sincere patriotic feeling towards their country, they realized the need to bear the responsibilities themselves in determining the country's future through friendly co-operation with others rather than dependence on outsiders.

When Britain decided to pull out, there were fears about the stability and security of the region generally and the anticipated power vacuum that might ensue. Bahrain had to make rapid strides in several fields. It had only a short time to prepare itself for the onerous responsibilities which awaited it after the imminent British withdrawal. It had to lay the foundations of a modern state which required a great deal of effort in the reorganization of various government departments and institutions functioning at that time and the preparation of the necessary cadres, both old and new, to fill the posts in various organs of state. All these matters were of the greatest importance. They claimed the total attention of our leader, High Highness our Supreme Commander, who issued sagacious orders for the building up of the state, basically relying on Bahraini citizens for this end. His Highness had implicit faith in their sincerity and confidence in their competence. He ordered the establishment of various state organs which absorbed a number of selected volunteers who were available to shoulder this responsibility from among the people of the country and others who were ready and enthusiastic to take up these tasks. The vacuum which was anticipated after the British withdrawal necessitated speedy solutions. High Highness the Amir called for the rapid formation of a military force which could both undertake the protection of the country and ensure its security and stability and also co-operate with its brother states in protecting the regions against various potential dangers, on the national principle of collaboration which united Bahrain with its Arab Gulf neighbours.

This happened when I was still at the military college, and I received the news with the greatest delight. I felt that the tough task I faced in my studies had become easy. The hardship and effort involved in training which I had faced throughout seemed to disappear. I was overwhelmed with joy at the thought of returning to my beloved country and once again being amongst faithful colleagues, devoted to their faith and homeland. I saw us all rallying under the flag of our beloved Bahrain for which we were ready to sacrifice our lives. It was my duty to work fast and I immediately started making plans, deciding on a badge for our military force and choosing its uniform without waste of time. I continued to ponder and prepare for carrying out the anticipated task in the near future during my period of study.

On 16th Zil Hijja 1387 H/AH 16 February 1968 I graduated from the military college and returned to my homeland. At the time no defence system existed except as an idea which required a great deal of study, experience and knowledge to implement. Before carrying out the project we had to lay down a sound basis and decide on the best means to undertake this great venture. The very nature of this task required starting from a point where others had reached their goal. We wanted quality rather than quantity of numbers as the guiding principle in the structure of our military force. The efficiency of the armed forces in the present-day world is no longer measured in terms of manpower but in its scientific capability and capacity to absorb the most advanced modern weapons and use them with maximum efficiency and effect. That was our concept of what we wanted to achieve and we were only at the beginning.

His Highness the Amir placed his confidence in me and charged me with the task of founding a defence organization for the state which was initially named the National Guard. An Amiri decree was issued appointing me as commander of the National Guard.

This appointment was made when I became the first military graduate and it helped me greatly in understanding what was required of me. It spurred me on to improve my knowledge so that I could shoulder my responsibilities as an officer who had been given the task of founding a military force in the service of our beloved country. A national guard in military parlance is taken to mean a seconding of defence in support of the regular armed forces and not a substitute for them. The armed forces are the bulwark of defence and the protective shield. From the outset the name National Guard was purely temporary. We were in a transitional trial phase when we wanted to know the extent of public response from the youth of Bahrain to the enlistment drive. During the last quarter of 1968 the doors were flung open for the enlistment of the first military intake in the history of modern Bahrain. The excellent results achieved exceeded all expectations as Bahraini youth came forward voluntarily in large numbers, spurred on by their faith in God and their country. By an Amiri decree the name was changed to the Bahrain Defence Force.

My faith in science and knowledge led me to pursue my studies further. In my capacity as the Commander-in-Chief of the Defence Force it was incumbent on me to achieve a military standard commensurate with my rank and position. It was my duty to set a living example to all ranks in the Defence Force. I had to encourage them to acquire knowledge and improve their military skills. Proceeding from this point of view I sought the permission of His Highness our Supreme Commander to attend a headquarters staff course conducted in the USA. His Highness agreed and I was able to do this in 1971.

At the beginning, the Defence Force did not occupy more than a single office located in one of the corners of the private Amiri court. While I was there, I was driven by an optimistic hope of performing my mission to raise a military force which was needed for the protection of our precious homeland. In one of the meetings with His Highness the Amir I expressed my desire to know what had been achieved in the military field by our brothers in Jordan under the inspiration of His Majesty King Hussein. His Highness immediately agreed forthwith and I made my first visit to the Hashemite Kingdom of Jordan during which I saw all the signs of the original Arab heritage with its resolution and spirit of co-operation exemplified in the personality of His Majesty the King. It was a good omen that I witnessed a victorious action over the enemy in the Battle of Karameh on 21 March 1968. This gave all of us a sense of confidence in our potential and in our determination to be victorious as an Arab nation if we could only speak with one voice and strengthen our military organization. I felt as if I were in my own country and I found many similarities between Bahrain and Jordan. The most important of these was the reliance of the two countries on their own manpower resources for their quality rather than numbers. We agreed to co-operate so that we could benefit from the military experience of Jordan.

The essential studies were made for the implementation of our plan. The first meeting was held under the chairmanship of His Majesty King Hussein, attended by members of the general staff of the headquarters of the Jordanian armed forces. In this matter, I would like to praise the spirit of co-operation and brotherhood which guided our relations with all officers of the Jordanian command and the support of His Majesty in making this co-operation a reality.

After I returned home, His Highness ordered us to commence our work. The training centre was also the headquarters of the general command. We decided to start turning out the first batch of officers and men. I must express the appreciation for the great influence that His Highness the Amir exerted through his material and moral assistance which helped us in overcoming the various difficulties and obstacles. One of the first of these measures of assistance was the construction of the necessary training centre. He also presented the quantity of small arms required for training the first intake of trainees. We started implementing the task without delay and thus launched ourselves on the first stage of founding a strong force. The confidence and trust which His Highness the Supreme Commander reposed in us, the officers and men, was an inspiration.

The beginning of the venture

The aim of raising the Defence Force was quite clear in the mind of His Highness the Supreme Commander as it was for me personally. The planning of this great national task was full of hope and it constantly occupied my mind. The basic elements for achieving the goal were derived from our past and present and we were spurred by our hopes for a bright future. I used to think of the best factors suited to our circumstances and in this way I gathered together all the important and effective elements in the task of constructing the force.

The necessary studies were undertaken in no more than three months. We produced an integrated plan for raising a defence force capable of defending our country and the achievements of our forefathers in order to provide our citizens with a secure, safe and prosperous life. The plan included all details and laid down priorities. The intention of His Highness the Amir to form a defence force was matched with a plan of action, and His Highness consented to its immediate implementation.

We started implementing the plan with great enthusiasm and in this task I was helped by a limited number of my colleagues. The work proceeded in accordance with a precise and simple plan.

I started issuing orders and guidelines and took the necessary decisions to raise the force and get it ready. I used to follow up all orders and decisions and in a period of no more than three months the training centre was ready, with the necessary equipment, training-grounds and stores. His Highness the Supreme Commander provided us with the small arms and vehicles which were required for the first phase of the establishment of the force. During this period rules were laid down for recruitment, funds were provided and military regulations issued. However, this was a continuous process and the issue of military rules and regulations of various kinds continued during the first three years of the life of the Defence Force. Thus we piepared everything and the training centre was braced to receive the first batch of recruits.

We had hardly started recruiting when the youth of the country came forward in such large numbers that I was overwhelmed with delight. How I wished we could take everyone who presented himself for interview before the recruitment board. The immense popularity of the recruitment drive left an indelible impression on my mind. One of the important elements of the plan was that the educated manpower of the country should be tapped and this was being amply achieved.

We started with the first batch of the first experiment with recruits. I wished it all success having prepared for it in every way. It was a nucleus of the force and its foundation. I realized that this batch would be a model of what was to follow in subsequent batches. Hence I was very keen on following its training programme. I supervised it personally until I became certain that the first military detachment which I longed to see on the soil of our beloved Bahrain would become a reality much faster than I had imagined.

I embarked on the phase of my life of practical service to Bahrain from the beginning of this period when I was the Commander in Chief. I commenced my actual military service with the first batch of recruits at the training centre. I acted as the commander of the training centre, followed the training programme and participated in its various activities in addition to what was required of me a commander-in-chief of the Defence Force.

During this period a number of young new colleagues joined us after they had completed their military studies. They were exemplary in discipline and readiness to shoulder responsibility and this increased my regard for them. I was happy with the spirit of co-operation which was displayed by all of them. They worked with an enthusiasm and sincerity which compelled admiration. The seamen's songs which they sometimes sang during work made me deeply aware of our adherence to our heritage and our values; as if they were reverting to the stories of our forefathers when they fought at sea. They had to be accustomed to life in the desert. This suggested to us that they should receive some training outside Bahrain. The Arabian Peninsula was suitable for this in the process of creating a sound military force and being able to bear the most severe conditions on land and at sea. We realized that the training of seamen to perform on land was easier than the training of infantry to work at sea.

Thus we learned many lessons. We took what we needed from our existing circumstances and adopted all that was new from which we could benefit. Our progress continued with the first batch with complete success. With the approach of their passing-out date, we started receiving the next batch of recruits. They repeated the splendid performance and many of them decided to enter this noble profession.

The time for the passing-out parade of the first batch was held under the patronage of His Highness the Supreme Commander. It was a historic and glorious day and I felt like the brother of those who were passing out rather then their commander. My heart swelled with pride and joy when I saw the graduates of the first batch carry out their functions with a high standard of excellence which could compare with advanced military institutions. They proved worthy successors to their forefathers and an ideal vanguard for subsequent batches to follow their example. In order to commemorate the occasion an Amiri decree was issued on 5 February 1969, declaring it the Bahrain Defence Force Day.

With the passage of time and with serious hard work many further batches of recruits passed out to increase our numbers. According to plan, the first three batches were combined to form a garrison infantry battalion which was prepared and equipped during the period of training of the first batch. It was natural that I should move my command headquarters to the garrison battalion. Thus I became the commander of the 1st Battalion. In addition to my being the commander in chief, I also supervised the establishment of the training centre which was filled with constant activity. We continued to take in further batches into the garrison battalion so that they could join the various groups and companies which had been constituted. At the same time the number of officers who were graduating from the military college and who had been selected for them at the outset was rapidly increasing. We also started preparing the cadres of non-commissioned officers with the first intake and trained them on special courses. With continuous work and effort I succeeded, with the grace of God, in completing the formation of the 1st Infantry Battalion and providing it with weapons, equipment and vehicles. We started implementing the special training programme for this battalion to gain experience and expertise and to prepare the first fighting unit ready to take the field in difference conditions of war according to the circumstances which might prevail.

Thus I constantly followed the implementation of the various phases of the plan with great confidence and for the third time moved to a temporary headquarters which His Highness the Supreme Commander had donated to our nascent force. It was a building which was being used as a guest-house. I started setting up the various branches of the General Command. The 1st Infantry Battalion was the source to fill the various gaps. This was in addition to some of our university graduates who had since been selected and received military training and appointed as officers to fill the administrative and technical posts at the various branches of the General Command. These branches started acquiring experience and knowledge with genuine enthusiasm. Very soon all branches of the General Command began to function competently which helped me to devote myself to the supervision of the training centre and the 1st Infantry Battalion.

During this period the various activities of the training centre and the 1st Infantry Battalion started showing results which increased my confidence in these dedicated people and my appreciation and affection for them deepened. We followed the progress towards the implementation of the remaining part of the first phase. We constituted fighting units, support units and administrative services and thanks to our continuous united effort and perseverance, we were able to complete all that we had planned for during this first stage. The Defence Force became a matter of pride to his Highness the Supreme Commander as it was to me personally.

First organizational outline for the Bahrain Defence Force

The following units are directly linked to the Command Headquarters of the Defence Force:

1 Training centre
2 1st Infantry Battalion
3 Armoured squadron
4 Wireless unit
5 Supply unit
6 Medical unit
7 Technical maintenance unit
8 Stores
9 Music

General framework for constituting the Defence Force

To everyone's good fortune the establishment of government schools in Bahrain started early in this century, i.e., more than sixty years ago.

74

This helped in providing scientific and cultural cadres for the country. This was considered a fundamentally important factor in the establishment of any operation which the country needed. When we thought of raising our military force, our first thought was of this broad cultural base which we found suitable for forming a modern defence system. Without hesitation they could learn how to use the modern weapons and equipment which we introduced. We had great confidence in the youth of Bahrain and in their enlightened outlook and self-discipline. This is what encouraged us to secure modern small arms for them initially, and then train them in medium weapons and later on the heavier variety. We struggled hard and continue our efforts to obtain the latest weapons and equipment most suitable for both conventional and specialized warfare. The availability of educated youth in our country made our job a lot easier. We now consider it our duty to provide them with opportunities to extend their education and knowledge and to offer them the leadership which they deserve having proved themselves worthy for the best kind of treatment.

It is sad that many people do not know the meaning of defence except in certain contexts. For instance, there are those who believe that the defence of the country means beating back any external aggression. There are others who believe that the defence of the country will enable them to advance themselves materially in an atmosphere of stability. There are still others who believe that extremism and seeking the assistance of various kinds of foreign forces will lead to the defence of the homeland.

I can think of many examples which will probably be contrary to some opinions but I shall confine myself to what I mean by the defence of the country. It is the defence of all that passed on to us in the way of values, heritage, our land which has provided us with its benefits, our faith in God and respect for man and the strengthening of national unity. Any neglect or compromising of our original values and their substitution with imported ideas and practices is, in my opinion, the result of a dangerous ideological imperialism which can only lead to chaos and ruin. We in the Defence Force feel proud when we repeat our motto with complete faith, 'God, Country, the Amir'.

Goals and principles

We do not have to think hard about the need for a Defence Force as all of us were already convinced of it. We realized that the time had come to set it up. This was one of the main reasons why we achieved speedy success in implementing the Amiri decree which laid down the principles and goals on which the Defence Force should be based and which are as follows:

- Protecting the independence of the country and preserving its security and sovereignty within its territorial frontiers and repelling any foreign aggression launched against it.
- Supporting the forces of internal security and assisting them in preserving stability and security in the country whenever needed.
- Joint Arab military cooperation.

The Defence Force consists of advanced regular forces in line with the requirements of modern defence.

In raising the force we followed the principles of self-reliance to the extent that was possible and co-operation with our brothers and friends in building up the force gradually. The challenge was great, but our determination, praise be to God, was able to meet it. Here I would like to record what I and all those gallant men who helped me went through in making our dream a reality of which we could always be proud. Our achievement was greater than can be described. This is only the beginning of our enterprise and a bright future awaits those who have the necessary determination. Next to God, I sought the co-operation of my brothers in arms to work with us with faith and confidence. Our goal is as stated before, through our work, sacrifice and dedication to return something of what we owe to our dear country.

Principles observed in the building process

In order to carry out our intentions, we took various decisions to provide the legal framework, and the military rules and regulations which are necessary so that every individual realizes his rights and duties. The duties, powers and restrictions laid down in the special rules and regulations of the Defence Force in addition to precise standing orders creating formations and commands make clear the duties of the individual and the extent of powers delegated to various levels of leadership and administrative cadres.

The implementation and application of rules and regulations enable every individual to bear his responsibilities and carry out his duties without confusion or ambiguity. This is a basic factor which governs relations between the men and those above them. If we work according to this system we avoid dealing with them on the basis of a centralized authority. In order to create a proper atmosphere for the performance of military duties a Defence Force Law was issued before the intake of the first batch of recruits which granted to the commander-in-chief the power to lay down rules, regulations and the method of recruitment. It also laid down the defined the rights of the members of the Force and their obligations. Thereafter, a special law was issued dealing with the conditions of service of officers laying down the procedure for their selection, training, assignment to courses, appointment, promotion and its conditions, transfer, secondment and retirement and their duties in all these cases. Later the law regarding men's service was laid down governing their recruitment, service, tasks duties and rights. In laying down the rules and regulations the principle of flexibility was observed so that they could be developed and adapted to suit the circumstances of the future.

I still remember the discussions that took place on the question of recruitment because there are two possible systems: one is that of compulsory national service or conscription and the other is voluntary service. The subject was brought up for discussion under the chairmanship of H H the Amir. We consulted some of the countries which had tried out both systems about their respective merits. Ultimately, we were convinced that voluntary service was more suitable for several reasons. The most important was that if we adopted the national service system we would not have the professionals to train the large body of men that would be involved. Moreover, a volunteer is an individual with motivation and his professionalism make him continue to serve and acquire expertise in his profession. This does not, however, mean that our minds are closed about the two systems. Whenever the need arises in future we may apply our minds to the problem afresh. In beginning with voluntary service we achieved unparalleled success in founding our Defence Force with great speed. Our enthusiasm impelled us to expand into the various fields of defence and to adopt the latest weapons for training.

We in Bahrain can never think of remaining isolated from the Gulf societies and the wider Arab national homeland while keeping in view our own psychological, economic, social, political and military potential. In this age no power can be self-sufficient in all respects. Its needs cover a wide field and they have to be met. Several reasons have contributed to this situation such as the wide range of modern weapons, and the speed of communications and movement. These days the world has shrunk. Hence we found it necessary to link ourselves with our brothers in the Gulf in a unified strategy and meet our obligations along with our other Arab brothers in this respect. No task, great or small, is without its difficulties or else there would be no challenges to face. We hope to co-operate with our brethren in facing these difficulties and overcoming them in order to reach our goals. At the domestic level every individual is quite clear about his own role and his potential.

With the grace of God we shall procure all our needs in the near future to be able to face various eventualities in different situations.

The educational background of individuals helps them to absorb modern military science in their fields of specialization or work. This science rests upon principles, concepts and various experiments recorded in thousands of manuals and books. However, any science can be simplified into two words; knowledge and skill. We should provide the individual with the knowledge he needs and then put him through his training so that he can acquire skill in the practical use of that knowledge.

Military science covers the basic principles of war. These are:

> Objective
> Offensive action
> Simplicity
> Unity of command
> Mobilization
> Economy of force
> Mobility
> Surprise
> Security

This is not the place to expatiate on these principles. However, with their efficient application and the main ones derived from them in all military operations we have achieved the aim of absorbing the essence of military science. Every principle of war can be applied in practice in many ways. Principles of war are one thing and the carrying out of unfamiliar military operations is another. This is where initiative and innovation come in. In short, military science is the best means of employing the principles of war. Moreover, military science is not isolated from the branches of knowledge which men seek. For instance, the question of the making of the qualities of a leader is useful at home and in society both during the period of service and after.

Those responsible for forming leadership cadres face several obstacles. We may recount our efforts in this regard. In order to achieve success in it we were always mindful as those responsible to be up to the level of our responsibilities. In this way we found that the superior and the subordinate should help each other in the cultivation of leadership qualities. It is difficult to analyse and define the art of leadership in words. However, we may say that like electricity, it is easier to explain its effects than the way it functions. The same applies to leadership qualities. A leader who understands human nature, possesses a marked personality and is equipped with above average knowledge and experience will always enjoy a greater degree of success and command the respect and appreciation of both his subordinates and superiors. A sense of responsibility is one of the basic characteristics of a good commander. In my understanding, a responsible person is one who starts by understanding himself with faith in his own role in his small family circle as well as in the larger extended family. Similarly he has faith in all the institutions which have been established to serve him. Thereafter he develops a kinship and identity with every such institution of which he considers himself a part in the public interest. Such a person does not need instructions and supervision.

He feels a sense of responsibility. This was most beautifully expressed by the Holy Prophet, who said: 'Each one of you is a shepherd and each one responsible for his flock.' In this lies the importance of leadership at all levels, it raises the standing of anyone whether he be of high or low rank. In raising the Force, we followed the principle of starting with leaders who possessed the following qualities:

- Capability of applying firmness, fairness and discipline in his dealings with his unit.
- Willingness to give an opportunity to subordinate commanders to display leadership in their tasks.
- Ability to determine objectives clearly and realistically within specific time-frames.
- Issuing orders in a military fashion; supervising the progress of work; guiding those who implement orders when needed; supporting competent subordinates; changing personnel who are not up to the required standard.
- Providing opportunities to every leader according to his aspirations and capabilities.
- Encouraging special skills and initiatives; recognizing any outstanding performance; granting special privileges appropriate to performance and showing appreciation for talent.
- Caring for the men's welfare and dealing with them as responsible persons who have their rights as well as obligations; creating mutual trust among all members of the unit.
- Providing the subordinate leaders with necessary information, informing them of the way things are progressing, and encouraging them to improve their general knowledge in addition to military science.

At the time of the formation of this Force we were training people from our own society in the technical and professional skills which are essential in running various kinds of plants and factories. Since the needs of the Defence Force were comparatively great and of various kinds we started preparing and training a considerable number of our men to be able to benefit from them during their service. At the same time we were joining other institutions in the task of training the professional cadres needed by the country.

The Defence Force is considered both complementary to the social fabric of Bahrain and inseparable from it. We took into consideration this basic and important factor from the moment we started thinking of raising a defence force since it was some of the youth of Bahrain who were to constitute the majority of this Force. The individual never loses contact with his social base. At an organizational level, the Command of the Force devised a policy for maintaining this continuity of contact by various means such as participation in national festivals by organizing fetes and military tattoos, and participating in the activities of civilian sports clubs, although most armies do not permit their men to have links with non-military clubs. All the same we encouraged members of the Force to continue contacts with their clubs as a measure of our support to these clubs so that they should continue to flourish. We have confidence that they provide support for our Defence Force. Such co-operation promotes pride among the members of the public in their youth even as it inculcates a sporting spirit among everyone. It is not unusual to see the captain of a team with the rank of corporal challenging a team with a lieutenant at the head. Similarly, the Defence Force maintains its links with civilian society by means of organized lectures and visits during which an exchange of information takes place and the citizens acquire a basic understanding of military affairs.

The link is also maintained by the Defence Force through co-operating with different ministries and public institutions in promoting general welfare such as in combating epidemics, helping in land reclamation and any similar projects within its capabilities. I fervently hope that these contacts with the general public will continue on a better and more organized basis in the social, cultural, sporting and other fields.

All this must be regarded as the basis of forming the nucleus of the National Guard at that time. Practical experience will provide new insights for those of us who never tire in trying to ensure a better future for our armed forces. We should support every proposal or study which helps to realize that noble objective. Here lies the importance of leadership which carries the responsibility for undertaking this exalted task while relying on the noble Bahraini citizen who has come forward to dedicate himself to the service and defence of his homeland. A wise leadership is one which emerges from trials with the smallest losses.

D The Defence Force and its Arab Role during the Ramadan War of 1973

What happens in our Arab Gulf generally and in Bahrain in particular may perhaps be obscure to many in our Arab nation. The Bahrain Defence Force had a role in the glorious Ramadan War of 1393 H/AD 1973 in accordance with the decisions of the Joint Defence Council of the Arab League. This imposed on our forces the task of supporting operations by maintaining a close liaison with the brotherly forces of Saudi Arabia should they have to enter the battle on the eastern front of the field of operations (Jordan) or on any other front under the joint command. On this basis we formed the first combat group for participating in this sacred duty.

In addition to our military role, the State of Bahrain had another role, in solidarity with other brother states, of reducing oil output and denying it to the states which were helping the enemy. This was beside the active moral and material participation of Bahrain at all levels from the Amir to the Government and the people. These are plain facts which are clear to everyone. These activities were backed by a morale of the highest level. We shall record these memories for history so that coming generations may find inspiration and enlightenment from them for the sake of our better future.

Let us look back a little and especially to the year 1967 when I was a student at a military college in Britain. At that time I was a young man full of enthusiastic faith in Arab glory. I had high hopes that I would see my brothers celebrate victory in the streets and squares of our Holy Jerusalem. Perhaps these feelings which had dominated my thoughts and fired my enthusiasm since my earliest days were one of the reasons which led me to enrol at the military college. What actually happened was the unexpected surprise of the calamity of 1967. British television showed us a military parade which was held in Jerusalem by our enemy. A sense of bitterness and sorrow shook me to the roots during my days at the college and thereafter.

After I graduated and assumed my responsibilities in the service of Bahrain, I started looking forward to the day when all Arabs would co-operate and collaborate in liberating the occupied lands. I was absolutely certain that the defeat would make every Arab realize his responsibility to undertake this sacred task in spite of the various challenges. In fact I would say that this matter dominated my thoughts at all times. When we were in the Command Headquarters of the Force we constantly analysed the reasons for the defeat and how we could best recover what had been taken from this nation whose past history was filled with actions of undying glory and outstanding military leaders.

Then came the Ramadan War of 1393 H/October AD 1973 which restored our faith in the values for which the Arab nation has been known by various peoples in its cherished history. This time the Arab soldier showed a new level of advanced intelligence. To his courage and skill he added the fresh knowledge of military science he had acquired. He demolished all the false propaganda about him by the Zionists after the defeat of June 1967. He taught the enemy a lesson which he would never forget. The great achievement of the Arab soldier during this war will remain a subject of study and inspiration for our immortal Arab nation.

When the war started, our recently constituted force was of very modest size and strength. In spite of this we sought to play our part. This had actually been one of the basic considerations in raising this force. When the time came, we consisted of the First Combat Group formed by the 1st Battalion and the necessary support elements. It was an important event because it was the first practical test of the fighting potential of our young force. This group had carried out various mobiliz-ation exercises in preparation for performing its future task. After the issue of the order by the Joint Defence Council mentioned earlier, the First Combat Group, after completion of all necessary preparations, was ready to be transported to Saudi territory and from there to the area of operations.

With their firm determination and high morale my colleagues responded in every way when I met them in the camp of the 1st Battalion while awaiting orders to join the battle. It was a very effective and decisive stand on our part. I should mention here that the average age of our officers and soldiers was about 30. While I was attending one of the meetings of the cabinet, the order to move was received. It was a historic moment which I recall with pride. I issued orders to the commander of the combat group to move. According to the plan the time required to reach the war zone was between 48 and 72 hours. When the combat group assembled in the concentration area, we received orders to stop because a ceasefire had come into force and hostilities had ended.

What was achieved by the Defence Force during the Ramadan War by way of mobilization, training and preparing for war with a high state of morale had its own reward out of all proportion to the youthfulness of this force which had barely been in existence five years. For me person-ally, our readiness to join the war and the heroism displayed by the Arab troops helped to heal the wounds of the disaster of June 1967. In this respect I would like to extol the effort put in by my brother and

1   H.H. Shaikh Isa bin Salman Al Khalifa, Amir of Bahrain.

2 Al-Rafa' Fort, built by Shaikh Salman bin Ahmad Al Khalifa in the nineteenth century AD.

3 Helicopters of the Defence Force patrolling modern Bahrain.

4   Al Hoora suburb.

5   Aerial view of the diplomatic area.

6   A further aerial view of the diplomatic area.

7   Ceremonial parade.

8   At the double.

9-14   Military training for every eventuality.

15 Gulf Cooperation Council Summit in Bahrain, December 1988.

colleague, the chief-of-staff, Major-General Khalifa Bin Ahmed Al Khalifa, who was the commander of the 1st Combat Group at that time and holding the rank of major when he accepted the responsibility for preparing the Force. He was eager, with his officers and men, to make any sacrifice needed for the defence of our honour and prestige. He had a very active role in the meetings of the Joint Defence Council and in the co-ordination of efforts between use and the Ministry of Defence for the brotherly Kingdom of Saudi Arabia.

E   The Role of the Kingdom of Saudi Arabia

When I try to recall all the factors which led to the formation of a relatively credible military force, the role played by the brotherly Kingdom of Saudi Arabia stands out. What the Kingdom did for Bahrain generally and for its Defence Force in particular is only a sure sign of the spirit of a single unified family.

It all started when my brother His Royal Highness Amir Sultan bin Abdul Aziz, Minister of Defence and Aviation, Inspector-General and Second Deputy Prime Minister of the Kingdom of Saudi Arabia, visited Bahrain at the end of the Ramadan War of October 1973. He made this auspicious visit without any previous arrangement and he expressed great appreciation for the Bahrain Defence Force's efforts to join the battle of destiny of the Arab nation against the Israeli occupation of Palestine. His Royal Highness indicated the readiness of the Kingdom to participate in building up and developing the Bahrain Defence Force according to the instructions he had received in this matter from the late King Faisal bin Abdul Aziz. His Royal Highness expressed great pride in the Defence Force and its high morale. He took the initiative in asking us what were our requirements. It was a pleasant surprise from His Royal Highness since the Defence Force was still in its early stages. In reply we informed His Highness of the plan which we had prepared for the development of our Defence Force which we had called the First Five-Year Plan. From then onwards we set out to build up the Defence Force as an integrated force which required both patience and perseverance.

The results of that cooperation began to bear fruit – including the supply of various equipment in addition to the strengthening of relations through mutual consultation between our two states. I can say with great pride that what was achieved can be considered a shining example for our Arab brothers, particularly the member States of the and thereafter to the wise Saudi command headed by the late King Faisal and later by King Khalid, may God bless them. We thank the Custodian of the two Holy Mosques, King Fahd bin Abdul Aziz Al Saud, who brought this co-operative endeavour to its full achievement.

In this respect I would like everyone to know that our goal is to co-operate with all our brothers in the Gulf region. With them we shall try to achieve complete co-ordination and active co-operation in the field of organization, weaponry, training and all other defence matters until we reach the intended goal which in the light of the guidance of our Amir is the defence of the Arab Gulf and the larger Arab homeland through a unified strategy.

F First Five-Year Plan

Introduction

The Arab-Israeli Ramadan War broke out in October 1973. The Bahrain Defence Force intended to participate in this war alongside the Arab Forces deployed on the Eastern Front. When the force was about to depart from Bahrain, an agreement was reached between the Arab and the Zionist forces for a ceasefire and we were asked not to move until the situation on the front crystallized further.

It became clear to us in the light of the task which we were to have carried out that there was a prime need to develop the Defence Force from a nucleus with limited potential to a well armed and well organized integrated force of all elements and to concentrate on improving its fighting potential and effectiveness to the highest levels. We started off forthwith and laid down an ambitious five-year plan after we had identified the areas of weakness and taken note of what was needed.

It was during those days that His Royal Highness Amir Sultan bin Abdul Aziz paid his visit to Bahrain as described above and expressed the readiness of the Saudi Kingdom to participate in the project of developing the Defence Force.

Aim of the plan

The development which we desired for the Defence Force envisaged close co-operation and co-ordination with our brothers in the Gulf region in the first instance and the purpose of our development plan was on the following bases:

- Raising the fighting efficiency and administrative and technical potential of the Defence Force.
- Achieving the required balance between the various weapons.
- Obtaining modern weapons and the latest equipment.
- Increasing firepower and mobility.
- Laying down new bases for advanced training and its development.

Support organization

The Bahrain Defence Force consisted, at that time, of small units of limited strength. But they were highly motivated and displayed great enthusiasm and determination to acquire the ability to handle the modern weaponry and equipment. In order to achieve the intended degree of development which we have referred to before, we were convinced of the need for a general reorganization of the Defence Force, keeping in view the following elements:

- Creating a general staff with various staff officers specializing in general command functions.
- Raising the level of the fighting units to battalion level.
- Increasing the potential of the support units to a high level of competence.
- Improving the administrative units so that they could serve all units of the Defence Force efficiently.
- Raising the level of weaponry in the Defence Force from small arms to medium and heavy weapons.
- The issue of orders for reorganization based on these considerations.

Implementation

At the beginning of 1974 the First Five-Year Plan for the development of the Defence Force began. Everything proceeded as planned and the Force was able, despite several difficulties, to achieve a great many of the intended goals. The main reason for this success was the continuous and colossal amount of work which was put in by everyone so that the reorganization covered all fields. The leadership of the Force was able very admirably to prepare the required cadres in the use of weapons and equipment included in the plan before they actually arrived. This made it easy for them to be speedily absorbed rather than dumped in the stores. As a result we always felt the need to avoid delays in obtaining our weapons. We overcame a number of obstacles to the implementation of the plan. There were several matters which were outside our control but which acted as a brake such as:

- Delay in the arrival of the required weapons and equipment.
- The control of the industrial nations which produced weapons and equipment over delivery schedules.
- Shortage of funds for certain programmes and projects.

The lessons we learnt in the course of implementation of this plan were of great importance. We kept these in view when we were implementing the Second Five-Year Plan and this enabled us to achieve far better results. We must praise the achievement of our Defence Force at that time when we held joint manoeuvres with the armed forces of the brotherly state of Saudi Arabia to assess the level we had reached in mobilization, administration and technical efficiency. The results confirmed our success in our task.

General repercussions of the plan at home and in the Arab world

The development plan generally received a wide coverage in the region. It was the subject of analysis and study in various quarters. At the local level, many comprehensive studies were made of the subject so that we could identify our aims and expectations. We wanted to know the economic and financial burdens which the state had to bear and what effects they would have on it. Ultimately the authorities decided to adopt the development plan *in toto* once they were convinced of the need for developing a Force which could perform its role of defending the country and ensuring its security and independence. It became clear to them that the Defence Force had a role in supporting the development projects of the State. The Force was considered an important source of craftsmen and technical personnel to take part in state projects. This would, in turn, accelerate the progress of the country in addition to the Force's contribution in various fields such as combating epidemics and diseases, cleaning up the environment, protecting the coastlines against pollution, launching rescue operations and carrying out various other tasks which need not be detailed here.

At the regional level some of our brother States expressed their total support and goodwill for the development plan which they thought would enable the Bahrain Defence Force to support and strengthen the Arab armed forces of the Gulf and actively participate in guaranteeing protection, stability and security of these various states which are bound by religious, national and historical ties and share a common purpose and destiny in the face of the dangers which surrounds the region.

G   Comprehensive Plan and the Creation of a Balanced Force

General

The recent wars have taught the lesson that the preparedness of the armed forces for performing the required duties effectively and competently rests basically upon:

- The competence of the leadership and its degree of control.
- Modern, developed weaponry.
- Organization characterized by simplicity and flexibility.
- A high level of education.
- Realistic and continuous training.

In the light of these lessons and as a result of what we learnt during the implementation of our First Five-Year Plan for developing the Defence Force besides other experiments we conducted during that period, our outlook assumed a deeper, more broadly based and comprehensive character. We increased our ambitions to raise the standard of our Defence Force. This required that we closely follow our progress in order to ensure integration and complementarity in the Defence Force and a balanced structure founded on modern, scientific and well considered principles. We took into consideration all the factors relating to the successful organization of any military institution.

The modern, developed weapons which have been acquired by the Defence Force and which will be acquired in future require us to review the organization of the Force so that it answers the needs of modern warfare under differing conditions and changing circumstances. We should provide an opportunity for the Defence Force to benefit fully from the characteristics of those weapons to enable it to implement the tasks allotted to it with total competence.

Factors bearing on organization

The organization of the defence force in any country depends on certain basic factors:

Nature of terrain

The nature of the terrain is considered one of the most important factors which determine the nature of the organization of the forces which are required to operate in the area. Desolate, mountainous terrain mainly requires infantry units or infantry carried in light personnel carriers capable of operating in these areas under various conditions and equipped with weapons which are suitable for the terrain and the country. Therefore, it requires the provision of basic means of transportation in its organization. However, in open areas the organization would require mechanized armour characterized by high mobility, speed and fire-power and capacity for shock action and also various means of intelligence-gathering and communications.

The nature of the ground in Bahrain is generally open. Hence the defence force here should basically consist of mechanized infantry with a high level of mobility, fire-power and manoeuvrability. In addition it should have some light armoured and amphibious units, with supporting artillery units and administrative units providing early warning and supervision.

It should be in a position to make use of air and naval weapons for locating enemy movements and confronting them effectively.

Nature of threat

The threat to be expected from the enemy is an important factor affecting the nature of the organization of the armed forces of any state. It requires an understanding of the aims and objectives as well as the forces of the enemy and his weapons, methods of attack and philosophy of war to have an opportunity to create a suitable force to confront him and deal with him successfully.

In studying this factor in relation to the organization of the Bahrain Defence Force, it becomes clear that it should be based on mechanized infantry with an emphasis on equipping it with the most advanced weapons including armoured and amphibious units in addition to fire-support and administrative units. These forces should be equipped with an efficient communications system and highly mobile mechanized vehicles capable of transporting them to the battlefield with maximum speed in order to grapple with the attacking enemy before he is able to establish a foothold on Bahraini soil. In addition, there should be effective naval and air forces to confront the attackers and hinder their advance. They should make use of early warning systems and observation for prior detection of enemy movements.

Manpower

The availability of manpower is a decisive factor in analysing the problem of organization of the armed forces of any state. General world standards have fixed the proportion of the armed forces to the total population in a country as varying between 3 and 5 per cent. These measures are also affected by age distribution and population density. In extreme cases the proportion may rise to 10 per cent or slightly more when a plan for mass mobilization in support of regular forces is adopted.

The importance of this factor is clearly noticeable in states with limited manpower potential. Bahrain is a state of this kind. It becomes clear that the Bahrain Defence Force should depend on modern and highly developed weapons to ensure the required level of fire-power while making up for deficiency in manpower. This requires continuous and advanced training of this force so that it reaches a high professional level for the optimum performance of its duties. Thus we make up in quality for what we lack in quantity.

Educational level

In the present age of scientific and technological development the available educated cadres in any state become a vital factor in deciding the nature, size and organization of the armed forces of the state. The illiterate or the backward no longer have a place. If we are realistic, we see that the state which achieves a high standard of education (such as Western countries, for example) basically depends on the invention and manufacture of modern, highly developed and complex weaponry so that it is able to equip armed forces who are of comparatively small numbers but who are educated and capable of absorbing and using these weapons with competence and ease. Thus these states ensure a qualitative superiority in their fire-power over their enemies. This, in turn, reduces the dependence on manpower which is a feature of several Eastern countries.

Since the State of Bahrain is small with a shortage of manpower and its people have a good standard of education which enables them to handle modern developed weapons, there is no doubt that the trend is towards organizing a military force of modest numbers but compensated by a very high standard of efficiency. This force has to be equipped with modern weapons and equipment to compensate for the manpower shortage.

Weaponry

Weapons are a factor of major significance in organization because of the impact of fire-power from a variety of weapons which may either destroy or neutralize the enemy. The basic elements in weapon systems are;

- target analysis
- data gathering
- means of delivery and launching
- transportation and movement capacity

In order to achieve the integration of any military organization the following should be available:

- Means of target analysis (air, naval and land reconnaissance and the use of radar).
- Means of delivering and launching at appropriate ranges combined with target analysis (land, naval and air forces).
- Accuracy, efficiency and density of fire-power with effective and destructive missiles (land, naval and air forces and air defence).
- Availability of means of transport (by land, sea and air) to ensure mobility.

It is clear from the above that there is a need for integration in the building up of the Defence Force of Bahrain and its organization in a manner which will guarantee its capacity to carry out its tasks in an effective manner. This is achieved by equipping it with a series of modern weapon systems and equipment (from small arms to rockets and aircraft) irrespective of the material costs and other economic difficulties. This is the only way to overcome shortages of manpower.

Economic conditions

The economic condition of any state is an important factor in the organization of its military force. Poor states which suffer from economic difficulties are not in a position to obtain modern weapons systems to develop their forces. Wealthy states, on the other hand, are in a position to obtain whatever they need in the way of modern and developed weapon systems which suit them even when they may not be able to produce such weapons themselves. Hence the economic condition of a state is a decisive factor in determining quality and quantity in the organization of its military forces.

The developing economy of the State of Bahrain, supported by the states of the Gulf Cooperation Council, gives it the capacity to develop its Defence Force as an integrated force, so that it may play a major role in helping the country to achieve its aims and to protect its security and independence. From this standpoint we did not find anything to hinder the implementation of our integrated plan for forming and developing the Defence Force in a comprehensive manner.

Climate and weather
Climate and weather are important because levels of heat and humidity, cold and rainfall help to determine the nature of the organization of the military forces of any country.

The climate in the region of Bahrain noticeably affects training, particularly in the summer months when the temperature hovers between 30 and 40 degrees C. It has an even greater effect on weapons and equipment because of humidity which sometimes reaches 95 per cent, requiring extra care and constant maintenance as well as repair of weapons and equipment. But, generally speaking, we may say that Bahrain's climate has a limited effect on the organization of its armed forces.

Principles of organization

General
The term 'organization' means forming a group of people for the purpose of carrying out a required objective with a division of responsibility for the performance of various tasks in a specified period of time. To achieve this a military organization should be characterized by a high degree of flexibility so that it is capable of assimilating a variety of weapons. The organization should be composed in such a way as to be capable of carrying out a task within a limited time with the least possible change in its basic structure.

The basic principles of organization may be listed as follows:

Unity of command
Unity of command here means that there should be a person in every establishment in the organization vested with authority to take appropriate decisions at his level. For every part of the organization there should be only one individual who is responsible. In practice this means that every person is responsible to his senior. The effectiveness of this principle lies in every individual knowing who his senior is and who are his juniors. An undesirable situation arises when an individual is held responsible to more than one person which in military parlance is termed duality of command. This leads to the individual receiving contradictory orders from his seniors. Which one of the orders is he

going to obey? The question may arise at a unit level where several units come under, say, formation 'M', which has full powers of command over them. Yet it would be possible to loan or attach such a unit to another unit. In such a case the unit to which it is attached acquires specific powers over it. In such circumstances, the senior unit which orders the attachment should lay down the extent of powers to be exercised by each organization – the parent organization and the unit to which the attachment has been made. All this led us to concentrate on the principle of unity of command in raising the Defence Force and its various units whether at the personal level of the individual or of units from the highest to the lowest.

Direct organization by the staff corps

Direct military organization by the commander and his staff corps, who are considered an extension of the commander, is a standard system employed by most armies of the world.

It is not possible either physically or mentally for a commander to collect all the required information bearing on a problem or a task, and to collate and sift it in order to reach a sound decision. The need therefore arose to create a staff corps in every formation to help the commander to take correct decisions.

The staff corps in any organization mostly consists of highly competent officers with a capacity to use scientific methods in solving the problems which face them. It is the staff who form a link between the commander and the units and they have the responsibility for assisting the commander as well as the subordinate commanders in carrying out the tasks delegated to them competently and in solving their problems.

We therefore had to train a number of our officers for this purpose and we sent them to various friendly and allied armies to attend advanced command and staff courses. This helped us to apply the principle of direct organization in the best possible manner.

Control

The extent and range of control is bound by the incontrovertible fact that a single individual can only effectively control a limited number of persons, say between three and seven. The factors which affect the range of control in an organization are the nature of the task and the time and distance involved. Where the task is simple and familiar, such as the pitching of a tented camp for a battalion, a unit commander can control from 10 to 30 persons.

However, in cases where a great deal of interaction between the members of the group and the leader is required, it is best if the group consists of no more than three to seven persons.

A commander is able, in most cases, to supervise the activities of his unit if these are confined to a single central area but the invention of nuclear weapons has led to the wide dispersal of subsidiary units. This limits the ability of the commander to exercise control over the activities of his subordinates despite the availability of modern means of transportation and communication.

Similarly the time factor is relevant in the range of control because of the time required for the orders to filter down through various channels of command to obtain the decision of the senior commander and for reacting to unforeseen situations.

All these factors require that we limit the chain of command to the minimum in organizing the Defence Force of Bahrain in order to achieve the best results.

Delegation of authority
The principle of delegation means conferring authority to persons in accordance with their responsibilities. When a task is allotted to anyone he should be given the powers he needs with sufficient freedom of initiative to implement it. If the powers granted are inadequate for the task, the individual is forced to refer to his senior for every decision. This naturally ties down the commander to various matters of detail and takes him away from tasks which are more important. In this type of situation the subordinate feels that his commander lacks confidence in him.

A commander who lacks self-confidence delegates additional powers to his subordinates to avoid taking the decisions himself. When a commander does that, he may be passing on to others extra responsibilities which he should have borne himself. The duty of a commander is to unify the efforts of his unit and guide them in the implementation of the tasks allotted to him. In order to achieve this he should exercise full ultimate control over the whole unit by himself.

We took this factor into consideration in organizing the Defence Force of Bahrain in view of its importance and its practical and moral effect on the officers and commanders at different levels.

Co-ordination
There is a natural centrifugal tendency in any organization and a desire for independence. Unless there is good co-ordination, individual units tend to erect an isolating wall around themselves. In essence the problem of co-ordination is one of marshalling various individuals within a single organizational entity for a correct and co-ordinated implementation of

the common aim with a minimum expenditure of energy and material resources. It requires applying the principle of total co-ordination between all the links in the chain or organization. This is what we took into account while organizing our Defence Force which now operates with a high level of co-ordination so that it has the capacity to fulfil its onerous tasks.

Flexibility

The principle of flexibility is very important. The organization should be flexible and simple so that individuals and units will find it easy to function in the midst of changing situations and circumstances. It is only a flexible and simple organization which will permit the combination or merger of units of various arms in order to carry out an objective easily and effectively without disturbing the basic structure of the organization.

We paid constant and considerable attention to this principle in organizing the Defence Force.

Balance

The principle of balance in organization is supremely important. It enable the integration of similar functions within the same framework. It applies both to units and individuals. With regard to similar units the task is usually of the same nature (for instance with infantry, armour, artillery, etc.). As for persons, their organization and assembly is based on different considerations such as the objective, time, place, etc. Many persons working in the same field of specialization such as finance or law, may be found in the same place or department where suck work is being carried out. The assembling of persons is done on the basis of the geographical unit whether it is the region or the country. Assembling depends on a time framework and a system of alteration.

The application of this principle helped us in raising the Bahrain Defence Force in a balanced manner including the various staff, and specialized branches to achieve the desired integration.

Relationship between organization, equipment and tactics

We had to study the relationship between organization, equipment and tactics because of their intimate relationship with the technique of organization. A military organization should consist of three major elements as follows:

Firstly, equipment: this includes the tools which are related to the tasks and duties which are required to be performed. The final goal of every military activity is the destruction of the enemy. In order to achieve this goal, the best means is the weapon. Hence the system of weapons should be modern and highly developed with the accent on their effective, professional and uninterrupted use. Military equipment, generally speaking, is divided into the following:

- Personal equipment which is intended to provide protection to the individual against the effects of weather and enemy weapons.
- Means of movement: these are the means of transporting units and persons for tactical or administrative purposes or for training, by land, sea or air.
- Means of communication: this is complementary to mobility and the use of weapons to ensure total co-ordination and control over the organization.
- Weaponry: weaponry is of prime importance among the equipment. Everything else is only to help in the effective employment of weapons. We have dealt adequately with the question of weaponry while discussing the vital factor of organization.

Secondly, the organization: the development of equipment leads inevitably to the development or organization from two basic angles.

- The development of equipment proceeds from the simple basic need for specialization. It is natural that the presence of special kinds of equipment should require specialists to operate them. The task given to any organization dictates the nature of its organization. The various weapons in a unit should be homogeneous from the point of view of range, communications, time of response, accuracy and manoeuvrability. This affects the extent of the organization because special and highly developed equipment requires an increase in the number of specialists at various levels.
- The armed forces are designed to obey the will of a single individual and to carry out his orders at all times. The organization of the armed forces becomes more complicated with an increase in their size and with the diversification of complex equipment. An increase in the size of the armed force poses several problems from the collection of information to the issue and distribution of orders. To ensure prompt response there is need for a chain of command from headquarters and staff corps in addition to standing orders for war and peace. Additionally there should be a unified system of training of a high order. Thus organization evolves as the size of the force increases.

Thirdly, tactics: the basic aim of developing the equipment and organization is to improve the chances of success in battle. The battle in itself represents a conflict between defence and attack. Therefore the relationship between the equipment, organization and tactics should be studied in relation to defence and attack. By defence is usually meant the prevention of the enemy from occupying an objective but an attack is launched to occupy a piece of ground or to destroy a body of troops or both at the same time.

Success in defence is achieved by the effective application and use of firepower whereas success in attack is characterized by continuity of movement and forward thrust until the objective is occupied.

Here lies the difference between defensive and offensive operations. An improvement in firepower and its effective use help defence, whereas an improvement in mobility helps attack.

For the organization to be sound and integrated it is necessary for it to be constructed to ensure fire-power, continuity of movement and the maximum manoeuvrability. This improves the chances of success in battle.

Methods of organization

A study of the factors which affect organization, its basic principles and the relationship between the organization and equipment and tactics make it clear to use that methods of organization differ according to geographical, human, cultural and economic factors and a country's state of scientific and technological progress. However, it can be said that a successful organization is one which is based on modern scientific and well conceived strategies which take into consideration all factors and principles for the organization to be realistic and capable of achieving its aims. It should have a capacity to carry out its allotted task in the best possible manner.

If we exclude the differences which arise from levels of scientific progress and technological development or from the geographical nature of the area of operations, most of the methods which are followed by different armies of the world have common features in their organizational structures. Organization at higher levels includes armies, corps and divisions.

The differences in organization at the divisional level, generally speaking, are attributed to the amount of firepower and logistical support available. Whether or not support is an integral part of the organization or attached to it will have a noticeable effect on its capacity to go into battle more or less independently. On the other hand, support may come through the higher command. These differences show up clearly in the methods of organization at a divisional or lower level as follows:

The army corps
This division is characterized by its ability to conduct operations in different stages of war comparatively independently because it has full fire and administrative support as an integral part of itself which enables it to perform its various roles. Fire support weapons, administrative services (artillery, engineers, wireless, supply and transport, medical, maintenance and repair) are all within the organization. An army corps can allot the necessary fire and logistic support units to its brigades to sustain their operations. The operation of an army corps is governed by several factors, including the extent of the field of operations, and the distances between the areas of operation of the divisions and its higher command.

An ordinary division
An ordinary division does not usually have fire support and administrative units as an integral part of it. Its organization is limited to its constituent brigades only. In its operations it needs to be allocated fire support weapons and the necessary logistic elements by its higher commander the general command. These are usually assembled with an ordinary division at the appropriate time. The weapons and logistic support are only put directly under its command during operations while they retain their links with their 'parent' corps for training, and 'technical' and administrative matters.

Brigade group
The organization of a brigade group is like an army corps in miniature and only differs from it in scale. A brigade group normally possesses fire-support and complete administrative support as integral to it and this enables it to conduct its operations effectively. This group may allot to its battalions such fire support and logistic units as they may need for their operations. The training and technical levels of the fire support and service units may be affected by the fact that they belong to other parts of the 'parent' corps.

Ordinary brigade
The organization of a brigade is a miniature of that of an ordinary division. In this case, the parent division of an ordinary brigade or the higher command bear responsibility for ensuring fire and administrative support for the operations of the brigade (that is grouping for a task force).

Battle group
A battle group is similar to a brigade group and consists of units of various arms to enable it to carry out its task efficiently.

Battalions/companies
A battalion is the smallest organization which consists of various fighting units which are self-sufficient to some extent as they have different types of weapons such as mortars, medium machine-guns, anti-tank weapons, guns and rockets.

Special forces
The special forces have a distinct type of organization, training and weaponry which enable them to perform special tasks that ordinary forces may not be capable of performing.

Ingredients of a successful organization

A study of the various factors, principles, and methods has shown us that the success of a military organization depends on the following basic elements:

- Firstly, leadership: This should be of a high order of capacity and effectiveness. It should be constantly enthusiastic in spirit. It should think deeply and lay down plans in advance to cater for different situations. It should take well considered and wise decisions and issue correct and clear orders. It should ensure that all tasks are carried out properly and with dedication. These are the principal factors which ensure success.
- Secondly, the staff corps: The staff corps should be attentive and persevering. It should consist of selected and competent officers who are noted for their initiative and energy. It should constantly seek means of improvement. It should aim to set standards and ensure the prompt implementation of the wishes of the commander. It should effectively assist the various formations and units to help them to overcome any obstacles which lie in their path.
- Thirdly, the forces: The units and formations should be comprehensively organized with all their needs of equipment and weapons. They should be self-sufficient from the administrative point of view and trained to professional standards. They should be constantly ready for battle and imbued with a high morale to perform their tasks successfully.

In view of the foregoing we may summarize the elements which contribute to success in battle between any two confronting military forces as follows:

- The size of the forces.
- The quantity of the equipment and its nature.
- The quality of the men.

The first two factors are self-evident. The third factor (i.e., the quality of men), is related to the art of leadership and the employment of troops and all other factors which affect the quality of leadership as well as of men. This factor is more important in a fast-changing situation. The basic requirement is that the individual should be of the highest standard to break the will of the enemy, overcome him and prevent him from achieving his objective.

These principles underlie the philosophy on which we built the organization of the Defence Force of Bahrain in whose development we have spent much effort, time and money so that it may come up to the expectations of our beloved country and merit its confidence through its preparedness smartness, initiative, and spirit of sacrifice. This is as the Lord says: 'Against them make ready your strength to the utmost of your power including steeds of war which will strike terror into the hearts of the enemies of God and your enemies'. (Holy Quran 8–60).

H   The Navy

During the various phases of its history Bahrain witnessed great naval and commercial activity because of its distinctive geographical position in the middle of the Arab Gulf and because of its important strategic position as a major link between the East and the West. For this reason Bahrain was exposed, like others in our Arab Gulf, to the covetous ambitions of foreign invaders who promoted various conflicts and rivalries in the region in order to dominate it and deprive it of its great wealth and prosperity.

The reaction of the people of Bahrain to these attempts has always been to confront the aggressor and sacrifice themselves in defending their land, religion and heritage. History tells us of various naval engagements fought by the Bahraini fleet in different periods in defence of the country, to preserve its security and stability and its wealth while ensuring safety and freedom of navigation for its considerable commercial fleet which carried a large variety of merchandise to and from Bahrain.

The people of Bahrain achieved great expertise in sea-faring from ancient times because they used the seas for trade, fishing and lucrative pearl-fishing. All these were a basic part of their pattern of life. Necessity drove them to take up ship-building both for commerce and warfare. They achieved expertise in this industry, excelled in the command and maintenance of ships and became indefatigable navigators by both day and night. They became accustomed to the ways of the sea and accepted its hazards. They learnt the various obstacles such as rocks, creeks and coral reefs as well as the sandy coastlines and safe anchorages. Through the leadership of their rulers who showed great initiative and wisdom they came to dominate the ocean. As soon as the Utoob, who included the Al Khalifa and the Al Sabah and those who followed them from the Arabian Peninsula to the Arab Gulf at the beginning of the twelfth century Hijra/eighteenth century AD, established themselves on its coastlines they started to build up merchant and naval fleets and they came to possess as many as 150 warships, with crews of 40 armed marines. Each warship had 3 guns (according to Ottoman document No. 111, page 713 dated 21st Rajab 1113 H, addressed by the governor of Basra, Ali Pasha, to the Ottoman Sultan).

Every emirate or shaikhdom in the Arab Gulf had its own naval and commercial fleet. The amir or shaikh was the actual commander of the naval fleet for it was an extension of his leadership over his tribe and the followers who lived with him on the island or in the desert. The amir or shaikh did not see any major difference between exercising his leadership in the desert surroundings of the past and the new environment of the sea to which they had migrated. The qualities of courage, self-sacrifice and initiative in confronting the enemy applied equally on land and at sea. The Utoob leader could command his naval force with the same degree of strength and skill with which he led his forces in the desert. He launched his war-fleet against the fleet of the aggressors with great determination of desert fighting.

The Utoob were able, in a very short time, to build towns and endow them with the aspects of civilization and culture. Both agriculture and trade flourished. The city of Kuwait was founded and then the township of Zubara which, during the reign of Shaikh Mohammed bin Khalifa Al Khalifa has recorded for us the names of scores of scholars who went there because they found security and stability under their wise rule. Shaikh Mohammed bin Khalifa Al Khalifa built a strong fort in Zubara with a turreted wall. He created a special entrance for ships to reach the fort under the supervision of a powerful defensive force. In this way the people felt secure. It helped in the establishment of schools and the expansion of trade. The ship-building industry and the repair and maintenance of ships progressed under the protection and guidance of an enlightened leadership. This secured for it the affection and loyalty of the people in their continuous progress.

When Nasr Al Madhkur, the then ruler of Bahrain, launched his attack on Zubara he failed because of the exceptionally courageous resistance put up by the people under the leadership of Shaikh Ahmed bin Mohammed bin Khalifa Al Khalifa which forced the attackers to flee. The dejected Nasr Al Madhkur who had suffered severe losses, fleet to Bushire instead of Bahrain, leaving his family in Bahrain. When Shaikh Ahmed advanced towards Bahrain to liberate it from the yoke of the Al Madhkur in 1197 H/1783 AD, he came to be known as Al-Fateh or 'the Conqueror'. This year thus marked the beginning of the liberation of Bahrain by Shaikh Ahmed al-Fateh who was welcomed by the Bahraini people as a victorious commander who released them from the clutches of foreigners who dominated the country and usurped its wealth.

That marked the dawn of a new era for Bahrain, of prosperity, progress and development. However, this did not last long as the foreign colonialist enemy, with the support of certain elements in the region whose interests were linked to those of the foreigners, began to interfere in the affairs of the Gulf to exploit its resources and destroyed the atmosphere of stability and fraternal co-operation that existed in the region. Enemy interference came in the guise of fighting the myth of piracy. I have called it a myth because it was a baseless fiction. The colonialists applied the term of 'pirates' to the people of the Gulf who were doing no more than defend themselves and their land. Properly speaking, a pirate is one who pounces on someone else in his own territory and deprives him of his livelihood. He terrorizes people who are attached to their own country. This description holds good for colonialists at all times and in all places. They never ceased plundering the wealth of the countries bordering the Gulf and then calling others pirates who usurped the Gulf for centuries. It was they who struck terror in its people, burnt their ships, destroyed their homes, harassed their shipping, and ruined their trade and pearling industry for years on end. This is what forced the people of the Gulf to defend themselves, their honour, their homeland and their possessions.

The Al Khalifa of Bahrain and Zubara rose as one man to defend their country and to repel the aggressors on each occasion. They strengthened and equipped their naval fleet and army. They enlisted brave men with a band of courageous leaders with a spirit of initiative. History has recorded their military skill in scoring successes in a series of engagements and their tremendous sacrifices to secure stability and independence for their country. This could not have been achieved without their determination and strategic planning even as they continued their military preparations in enlisting men, strengthening the fleet and training their people to defend their land.

Their interest in creating a war-fleet was dictated by the country's historical circumstances over a number of years. The ruler of the country was also the commander of the fleet as we have said before. The situation continued in this way until the arrival of the British in the Gulf. They tried to liquidate the naval fleet entirely and were largely successful because the Gulf was left with nothing with which to defend itself. When the British withdrew from the region this was the situation that existed. The present is to be considered as an extension and continuation of the past. On this basis we set about building our navy with the goal of achieving a well balanced Bahrain Defence Force equipped to defend the country and co-operate with our brothers in the Gulf and the Arabian Peninsula in defence of the region as a whole against avaricious enemies.

CHAPTER 4

National Strategy for the Gulf Cooperation Council States

Introduction

1   The comprehensive cultural development of society is based on an effective mobilization of its potential to achieve the fullest and optimum interaction between manpower and material resources, religious, spiritual and cultural values and lastly the ability of an enlightened leadership to exploit all the potentials, mobilize them and organize the synthesis between them.

2   The act of mobilizing a full synthesis between the potentials of a society is achieved through a whole range of organizational systems. The value-based cultural framework which provides the essential ingredients of cohesion and identity in a society with its linkage between its past and present, is the starting-point for progress towards the future. It manifests itself in the political framework at the higher level for taking decisions, determining priorities and goals and distributing resources within the society according to a general policy. The selection of a course within a strategic framework and the most suitable way of implementing political decisions, derive from a realistic appraisal of facts in relation to aims and objectives. The framework of planning is represented by the institution entrusted with the task of translating the goals and priorities laid down within the political framework, and determined according to the overall strategy. In turn this is converted into programmes and projects with their allotted time-frame and the required material, manpower and organizational resources are allocated to them.

Then comes the phase of implementation with all the technical details for each sector and the necessary system of co-ordination and follow-up action and the provision of means and materials. This framework depends on the administrative and technical organs of governments as well as private sector agencies and institutions. Then comes follow-up action with corrective measures through the assessment of qualitative and quantitative results achieved compared with the established planning goals so that the necessary modifications are made in the means and methods of execution. This enable one to benefit from the final results as a whole while laying down general and sectoral plans for the future.

3   These remarks about the framework of development of society shows that the national strategy of the GCC states represents the sum total of thinking required to determine the best course for achieving the comprehensive cultural development of the Gulf society. This strategy is based on a comprehensive view of the conditions and characteristics of Gulf society within the framework of internal and external variables as well as on defining the final goals and the principal means of achieving these goals. It relies on an appreciation of directions it is likely to take in the long term. In this respect it marks a phase of transition from higher policy decisions to one of specific planning for objectives and mobilization of resources.

4   The success of the strategy and its effectiveness in achieving progress and development for Gulf society depends on a combination of the following factors:

(a) Complementarity and comprehensiveness in planning a strategy. This requires that the strategy is laid within an integrated framework of political, military, economic, social and organisational elements.

(b) Preparation of a programme of work to translate the generally defined strategic goals of strategy into subsidiary goals at the Gulf level and the level of individual states of the GCC. It should lay down the basic tasks for achieving all goals, the order of priorities, the required potentials, methods of execution and the necessary time-schedules for implementation.

(c) An agreement between the GCC states over the ideological framework through which a consensus can be arrived at about a set of principles, goals and responsibilities needed to implement the strategy. Success in laying down a national strategy cannot be achieved if we become prisoners of thought, refusing to innovate or change, or if we continue to think along the pattern of advanced industrial states. Thus a national strategy requires innovation and fresh thinking in conformity with existing realities within the mould of an integrated culture. It should have a clear identity and individuality. It should be well defined with regard to the type of society we aspire to, within the context of its political and economic goals and its fundamental social values, as well as to the general basis for the system of government. It should define the rights and obligations of citizens and the way of life and outlook we aspire to for the Gulf citizen.

(d) A total commitment to agreed objectives and strategy among the GCC states. One should act in the interests of the GCC states as a whole and override sectional interests of an individual state. One should stoutly reject the pressures arising out of limited local conflicts. Any fears and suspicions about the procedures adopted for the realization of strategic goals should be replaced by confidence.

(e) In determining aspects of strategy one should rely on the general goals of the GCC. The Unified Economic Agreement should be considered the basic channel for defining the ingredients of this strategy.

5   In the light of the concept of strategy outlined above and within the framework of the relevant factors we shall review in subsequent sections the national goals of the GCC states, the nature of the risks and threats faced by them in the political, military, economic and social fields and the concept of a deterrent strategy to meet these threats.

A   National Goals of GCC States

1   The Charter of the GCC of the Arab Gulf states has defined the main goals to which the Council is devoting its energies.

2   The final communiqué of the sessions of the Higher Council of the GCC states and the working paper dealing with joint Gulf action have incorporated the decisions approved by the Higher Council in its first session about the general policy of the Gulf states within the framework of the following national goals:

A   The achievement of security and stability in the Arab Gulf region, defending the GCC states and protecting their independence and political systems

1   The final communiqué of the first session of the Higher Council of the GCC referred to this general goal and outlined that Their Majesties and Highnesses had reaffirmed that the security and stability of the region is the responsibility of these states and their people. The GCC of the Arab states of the Gulf expressed the will of these states and their right to defend their security and independence. It reiterated their absolute rejection of any foreign interference in the region whatever its source. It demanded that the region be kept away from international rivalries and particularly opposed the introduction of foreign naval fleets and the introduction of bases. This was in the interest of these states as well as of the well-being of the world. Their Majesties and Highnesses emphasized this general goal in the final communiqués issued at the end of the second, third and fourth meetings of the Higher Council of the GCC.

2   The working paper on Joint Gulf Action included a reference to 'the fact that this age is inclined towards the formation of large political and economic entities in order to ensure stability, security and progress and avoid the errors into which many states in other parts of the world have fallen and had to pay a heavy price in terms of blood, men and money. These errors arose from unending and indecisive regional conflicts which sapped their energies and inflicted heavy losses on many people.'

3   If the challenges are enough to induce active co-operation in any region of the world then the circumstances prevailing in the Gulf region are especially conducive to this end. Here we constitute parts of a single nation bound together by one religion, a common cultural heritage and shared values and customs. In view of our geo-political location and oil wealth which render us susceptible to international political avarice, or even blackmail, we are driven even more towards joint co-operation.

4   The working paper referred to above added that the challenges faced by this region were accentuated because of the great need of the industrial world for oil. This made the Gulf merger a vital factor in giving it a new sense of direction and a political, economic and social content to keep the regional away from international rivalries and avoid it becoming an object of competitive bargaining. International rivalry cannot affect a united region which speak with one voice, has one opinion and

has a united force. On the other hand greedy power can find a thousand ways of intervening in the area; rich in its oil and its people, it is fragmented into small units which can easily be penetrated.

5 The talk about a power vacuum in the region rich in wealth but without owners in control will end if the masters of their own house play their collective role with determination and steadfastness.

6 This indicates that the overall policy of the GCC states in the political and military fields rests on the following foundations:

(a) The effort to achieve security and stability in the Arab Gulf region is vitally linked to the preservation of the independence of the GCC states and their political systems. Both of these elements constitute a balance which will be damaged if there is foreign interference or if the potential for defending the GCC states and preserving their independence and political systems is lacking.

(b) The security and stability of the Arab Gulf region contributes to the achievement of world peace. This peace depends on a conscious understanding by the great powers that the inescapable need of this region is to be kept away from international conflicts, rivalries and ambitions. This alone will enable the GCC states to play their role in strengthening the world economic system and in helping to achieve prosperity for all people through cooperation with all international forces and establishing equitable relations with them in accordance with their attitude towards the GCC states.

The creation of a balanced and integrated social background

1 This objective is embodied in the effort to achieve comprehensive development ensuring economic prosperity to satisfy the material needs of the people. This is to be achieved by the development process and the diversification of the overall sources of revenue of the GCC states. This will improve the potential of these states for providing the spiritual, social and cultural needs of their citizens, changing undesirable patterns of behaviour and social relationships and replacing them with positive and reliable values in harmony with those prevailing in the civilization of the Arab Gulf. This will change other values which may impede the development process apart from their economic and social aspects.

2 The working paper dealing with joint Gulf action emphasized the importance of integration and balancing the development process. This

is the objective for which the GCC states have made themselves fully prepared to achieve. The paper referred to 'the difficult and real task which faced them all which made it inevitable that they should address themselves to the tasks collectively. They depend on oil which is an expendable commodity although it generated considerable wealth during the last 10 years. At the same time it also created severe strains and brought about changes in human behaviour. The people of the Gulf today look to their governments for a solution to the difficulties they face of achieving real and continuous development on the one hand and preserving social stability, peace and progress on the other. This problem could never be solved without a deep understanding of the priorities which are the establishment of the basic infrastructure and a firm production base on the one hand and the preparation and training of the precious commodity which is the human potential on the other. They should face up squarely to the important question of how to convert oil into comprehensive and stable development in the interests of their people.'

3 It becomes apparent from this general aim that the broad policy of the GCC states in the economic and social fields should be on the following bases:

(a) The distinctive characteristic of the GCC states compared to most developing countries is the availability of the necessary funds for comprehensive development. It enables them to acquire essential prerequisites for the implementation of various economic and social programmes and also enable them to use modern technology in modernizing the means and methods of production and expanding the available potentials. This characteristic of the GCC member states, in addition to what has already been achieved by the mere establishment of the GCC in providing the political will, makes it possible for them to adopt joint decisions and policies. The policy of self-reliance in achieving economic and social goals and confronting the problems arising from them becomes feasible. This requires that we abstain from merely copying the methods employed by other developing societies in the past because their circumstances, resources and value systems were different from the realities of the Gulf in the same context. We have to rely on initiative and innovation as a prerequisite for a sound development plan for the GCC states in cooperation with one another. Moreover, they should benefit from the lessons learnt by others in order to modify the economic framework of the Gulf and its position within the world economy by departing from the routine process and basing development on a foundation of independence and self-reliance.

(b) The aim of development in its cultural context is to make the dignity of man a matter of prime importance and to act to satisfy his ever increasing spiritual, material, social and cultural needs. He should be reassured as to his present and future condition. The human being is, at the same time, both the architect of this development and its prime motive force. It is only with his effort and his abilities that he can achieve it and ensure its continuation. It means that this basis of development is the introduction of the human element in all its efforts. These efforts should not be restricted merely to the aspects of economic development, capital formation and the increasing of gross national product.

(c) The development process of the GCC states certainly offers an opportunity for citizens to participate both in the effort and in reaping its rewards. This desirable participation is required in organization and the laying down of the necessary planning policies, the formulation of objectives and clarification of the choices available and the adoption of decisions about distribution of responsibilities in the implementation of the plans and programmes. Participation is also required in sharing the advantages achieved from the various activities, within the framework of social justice and equality, in the provision of opportunities in life and in expanding them for all citizens whatever their place in society.

(d) A balanced combination must be made between the values of our heritage and the current and future realities of the surge of development in the GCC states. This requires a close examination of the facts, and of the direction of development until we reach the essential roots of our past heritage as well as our present problems so that we may continuously attain both our more immediate and our distant goals. We can do so with complete confidence by making the necessary decisions and selecting the appropriate means based on spiritual and religious values embodied in our cultural heritage which represents a major source of strength in confronting contemporary challenges.

(e) The Unified Economic Agreement among the member stages of the GCC represents the general framework of the policy of Gulf economic development.

C Strengthening the reality of Arab and Islamic identity

1   The Charter of the GCC states has emphasized that conformity with the Charter of the League of Arab States, which calls for stronger and closer relations between members and directing efforts towards strength-

ening and serving Arabs and Islamic causes, is considered one of the main justifications for the establishment of the Council.

2   In the concluding statement of the first session of the Higher Council of the GCC states, Their Majesties and Their Highnesses emphasized their adherence to the Charter of the League of Arab States and the various resolutions issued by the Arab summits and renewed their commitment to the Islamic Conference resolutions. The working paper concerning Joint Gulf Action pointed out that Arab unity, ever since the dawn of Arab independence at the end of the Second World War, has remained the objective of all Arab people and the time had come now to adopt positive steps in this field. This was a region which embraced Islam, nurtured Arabism, and has been imbued with concern for interest of the nation since the dawn of history. The member states of GCC as a whole are capable of making themselves heard in the councils of the world as well as in their region, asserting their position in the world economy and emphasizing their active role in espousing Arab causes.

3   *This general goal points to the fact that the general policy of the GCC states at the Arab and Islamic levels is based on the following principles*:

(a) the establishment of the GCC is not a political grouping or a military axis directed against anyone. It is in fact a framework for co-ordinating the various aspects of the co-operation which has existed for a long time among the member states of the GCC. It aims at joint effort for strengthening this co-operation at the Arab and Islamic levels so as to reinforce the Arab national entity and serve the interests of Islamic states.

(b) The internal leadership of the GCC states and their efforts to achieve a complete and balanced development proceed from the goals of joint Arab action and represents a cornerstone of Arab economic and social integration.

(c) Integration between regional Gulf action, national Arab action and Islamic action springing from religious commitments is a basic element in the policy of the GCC states. The contemporary Arab has no civilization and culture divorced from Islam; it is a fundamental element in the civilization of the Arab nation. There is nothing in the tenets and principles of Islam to prevent a political movement in a nationalist trend in response to outstanding interests, neighbourly obligations, sharing the same language and preserving joint Arab security. The strengthening of regional societies through various forms of co-operation and unification also strengthen Arab societies as a whole which in their turn strengthen Islamic societies.

(d) Building up a technological capacity appropriate to the circumstances and the needs of the GCC states:

(1) The Charter of the GCC states refers to the fact that stimulation of scientific and technological progress in the fields of industry, mining, agriculture, water resources, animal husbandry and the establishment of various centres of scientific research remains one of the main aims of the Gulf states. The fourth chapter of the Unified Economic Agreement contains the details of various means for realizing this goal.

(2) This aim refers to the general policy of the GCC states in the field of science and is based on the following foundations;

(a) the problem of development in the GCC states does not depend for its solution on the mere transfer of the latest technology and its employment in the various development programmes. What is needed is the selection of technologies which are suitable for the states of the region from the viewpoint of their effectiveness, the size of the market, the type of worker required and the extent of institutional support and technological know-how which is locally available to operate and maintain the system. This is in addition to the problems of competent handling of instruments of technology within the cultural and social framework of the GCC states.

(b) It is necessary to function in a way that experience and know-how in technological fields is developed in the course of the operation in partnership with foreign institutions for this is the key element in the import and transfer of technology. It becomes essential to develop technological cadres at different levels and to provide them with all the necessary equipment and ensure their protection.

(c) The employment of technology is not restricted to the economic aspect of the development process but also extends to the social aspect. This requires that the use of the latest technology in harmony with the content of the cultural values of the GCC states. Similarly, it is necessary to control and contain certain negative results which may ensue. It will also entail the establishment of organizations and institutions which are efficient and suitable and to develop human behaviour patterns and trends which will make the introduction of new instruments of technology yield both economic and social results Similarly, it is necessary, in the fields of culture and information, to select suitable material which keeps in view the aims of development in the GCC states and adapting it in such a way that this material is produced indigenously.

B   Dangers and Risk Factors Faced by GCC States

General

The appearance of oil marked a strategic turning-point in the evaluation of the strategy of the GCC states because they became the centre of attention of all states which needed their oil much more than they needed strategic control over their region. Therefore, there has been much discussion over the past decade of the question of 'Gulf security'. This term has been given different connotations by different parties in accordance with their various interests.

On the other hand, the oil wealth and the increasing accumulation of capital which this has generated has also created a number of economic and social problems in the development pattern which the GCC states have adopted in building up and modernizing their societies. This section outlines some of the dangers faced by the GCC states. As far as possible these are classified according to their political, economic, military and social dimensions. Some of the threats faced by the GCC states are of a composite nature in which all these dimensions above interact to pose dangers of external hostility, of glaring maldistribution of income among various social groups and the danger posed by the increasing presence of foreign labour, etc.

This chapter discusses the following threats: the political threat; the economic threat; the social threat.

The political threat

1   *Increasing International Rivalry in the Arab Gulf Region*
(a)   The United States looks at this sensitive and vital region of the world in terms of the US economy in particular and the security of the Western world in general. This is because this region produces 70 per cent of the oil needs of Europe, 85 per cent of the requirement of Japan and about 30 per cent of US needs. The interests of Western oil

companies are no less important than those of the consumer countries. The extent of these interests is represented in the size of the investments and profits they generate. From the Western point of view, Gulf security means the security of oil supplies. On 23 January 1980, US President Jimmy Carter declared: 'Any foreign attempt to gain control over the Gulf will be considered an attack on the vital interests of the USA and all such aggression will be resisted by all possible means including military options.' The United States constituted a Rapid Deployment Force which has now become a full-fledged army of 400,000 soldiers under a central command. It has secured bases and military facilities in Egypt, Somalia, Djibouti and the Indian Ocean – a development which emphasizes the determination of the USA to confront any attack in this region as it considers it to be the first line of defence, in the words of the US Defence Secretary. On the other hand, the American support for Israel and the signing of a strategic co-operation agreement between the two will compel the USA to extend aid to Israel including the provision of all possible intelligence about the Arab Gulf regions and its defensive capability and economic potential.

(b) As regards the Soviet view, former President Brezhnev had announced a Soviet plan consisting of several points, including an important proposal for the neutralization of the Gulf, by which he meant the insulation of the region from American and Western influence in general. This would have enabled the Soviet Union to gain a foothold in the region, a Russian objective since the days of the Tsars. It aimed at securing a naval outlet to warm waters and gaining control over the bottleneck of the Western economy at the Strait of Hormuz. The Soviet Union had continuously striven to acquire allies in the region by offering military and economic assistance to some states and following it up by imposing its control through establishing military bases and signing friendship treaties which in reality were military alliances with states which entered its political orbit. Similarly through the armed invasion of Afghanistan, the Soviet Union aimed at reaching the Gulf waters and establishing a foothold in this region by which it could threaten oil supplies to the West. The Soviet Union constantly aimed to strengthen the institutions and fronts which had been established in the states and were subserviant to it in order to operate against the GCC states. We have to remember that it is always possible that Russia, the Soviet Union's successor, will show interest in the Gulf region in the future.

2 Neighbouring aggression
The ambitions and aggressive postures of some states in the region, including Israel, aim to weaken the Arab nation militarily and economi-

cally and divide them and prevent them from acquiring modern technology. They look with alarm at the continuing development of the Gulf region and hunger for its vast resources.

3 Arab differences
Inter-Arab differences and conflicts have wasted considerable energies and resources of the GCC states and damaged them politically and militarily from the time that these differences have had a military content rather than reflecting merely propagandist and political positions.

The economic threat

1 Absence of the concept of economic planning and programmes
The absence of economic plans covering the various sectors in some of the GCC states has led to wide fluctuations in the levels of economic development, the dissipation of considerable material resources and total subservience to international market forces.

2 Continued reliance on oil as the main source of economic activity
The danger arising from the continued dependence on oil lies in the possibility of total economic stagnation for the GCC states in the event of a halt in production or a collapse in prices.

3 Unstable role of the services sector in diversifying the sources of income
Lack of stability in this sector and its unreliability in diversifying the sources of national income are linked to the internal political situation and external threats. Without direct state control over the development of the services sector, it is impossible to pursue the strategy of diversifying the sources of income in the case of any internal disturbances or external threats leading to the flight of this sector outside the country.

4 Doubts about the process of industrialization
The process of industrialization in the GCC states was affected by many doubts and negative factors which resulted in a lack of clear industrial planning policies. The following are some of these negative factors:

(a) An increase in the cost of establishing and operating factories.

(b) The lack of the basic infrastructure for industrialization in the GCC states. For instance, there is a lack of a tradition of industrial production and marketing an an unwillingness to accept the consequences of industrial life – in particular a sympathetic consideration of the worker's needs and his social and political ambitions.

(c) The reliance of industry on petrochemicals and hence the suscepti-bility of all other economic secrets to any recession in this industry.

(d) Subordination to foreign control due to dependence on external markets for the distribution of industrial products and for the obtaining of raw materials, technology and labour with an increasing danger of such subordination when the various horizontal and vertical links in the process of industrialization are weak.

5 Fluctuations in financial policies
This phenomenon is related to the policies of some GCC states which fix their level of expenditure in relation to their anticipated income rather than to what is essential. This carries the following economic risks:

(a) A lack of reserves to enable future generations to maintain eco-nomic standards when the supply of oil as the basic economic com-modity is reduced.

(b) A constant increase in extravagant and wasteful over-expenditure.

(c) The appearance of various economic bottlenecks, leading to specu-lation and improper investment.

(d) An increasing reliance on imported manpower.

6 Absence of clear investment policies
The GCC states suffer to various degrees from a lack of clear-cut invest-ment policies based on the allocation of a specific proportion of national income to investment and current expenditure. On the other hand, the investments of certain GCC states are exposed to the political threat of their being confiscated in the event of international tensions arising in some other states. This is due to the lack of diversification and maldistribution of their investments.

7 Negative factors which affect progress towards economic co-ordination
These factors are as follows:

(a) Those which arise from the maldistribution of income among the GCC states which causes a lack of homogeneity between members of the Council and disparities between their citizens which make it difficult to deal with each other on a basis of equality.

(b) Weakness in the development of joint projects among the GCC member states, particularly in matters concerning the location of projects on political considerations which have insufficient justification on serious, economic grounds. This results in a lack of enthusiasm to see to their completion.

(c) Contradictions between the general interests of the member states of the GCC based on the Unified Economic Agreement and the special interests of some GCC states.

The social threat

1 Citizens' participation in framing general policy
The feeling among some citizens of the GCC states that they are not participating in the formulation of their general policies has resulted in their following negative trends:

(a) Withdrawal of a large number of GCC citizens from the mainstream of life as they confine themselves to pursuing their personal interests.

(b) A weak sense of identification with society, a reduced social consciousness about the reality and importance of the projects for development of their active participation in their execution.

(c) The delays in implementation of various projects, the heavy material losses incurred, increases in costs of production or a decline in quality in addition to increased expenditure in the administration of social, health and educational services.

2 Loss of balance between the rate of economic development and the nature of social change
This occurs when there is a high level of economic development while the necessary accompanying social changes in the adoption of behaviour patterns and avoidance of undesirable social relations are neglected. This gives rise to the following negative factors:

(a) A weakening of the value of individual participation in the development of society and reliance on the state to provide for all needs. This generates a general feeling that social reform is the responsibility of governments, that they should be capable of effecting all changes and bear responsibility for providing all services. They are held responsible for the prevalence of illiteracy and for the lack of awareness of the meaning of responsibility, co-operation, common action and consultation.

(b) The absence of the concept of public service among some employees of the administrative system who tend to deal with the general public as if from a position of higher authority enjoying certain privileges and deciding peoples' interests, has led to an unhappy relationship between the government and the people. In addition the feebleness of the concept of public service among the youth of the GCC states has led them to become either purely self-centred or to despair of any kind of reform and see a role for themselves in reform.

(c) Lack of appreciation of the value of work among certain social groups arising from a feeling that absence of any need to work is a symbol of high social status. Such people look down upon and belittle manual or professional work and adopt an air of superiority over their friends. They look upon work as if it were only a means to acquire wealth. Thus there is a loss of balance between the rights and duties in certain aspects of employment relationships.

(d) Lack of awareness of the value of time in daily life, lack of discipline and precision in work, lackadaisical performance and minimum levels of effort.

(e) Poor observance of rules and regulations either out of a lack of belief in their fairness in general or because of the society which does not bother to obey the requirements of the law and the exemptions to its general application. In addition there is an inadequate effort to educate citizens about their fundamental rights and duties as laid down in various laws.

(f) Weakness in the role of women in social life whether it concerns the supervision of the family or her participation in all phases and aspects of the development plan either because of established custom or because of a certain mistaken notion of incompatibility between the role of a woman in society and the essence of Islamic teaching on the subject.

(g) Fanatical adherence to certain concepts of ancient tradition. Some people are frozen in their present situation which is tied to the past. This is due to lack of clarity of the meaning of heritage. The past is not sacred in itself but is important in as much as it can provide us with guidance and direction. The accent should be on the present which is our field of operation. The future is still awaiting us and nations which try to shape and influence history should prepare themselves psychologically for their progress towards it.

(h) The readiness of some educated people to accept concepts and views which are prevalent in the West or originated there. They look at the culture of their society through Western lenses and attempt to reform it in the light of Western values which are totally divorced from their own prevailing concepts of culture.

(i) The emergence of fundamentalism and religious bigotry which adopts harsh and rigorous practices for itself and imposes them in matters of worship and mutual dealings while accusing contemporary Islamic societies of ignorance.

(j) Devotion to consumerism, extravagance in spending and ostentation on social occasions such as marriages and birthday celebrations. This phenomenon has almost become a pattern of life as a result of the sudden change from limited national income to prospects of vast wealth. Some people have been exposed to sudden psychological pressures because of marketing techniques and sales drives for consumer products of international companies. Individuals and families tend to be affected by these trends.

3 Shock of development
The speed of development witnessed by the GCC states during recent years while various aspects of traditional life or inherited tradition remain has administered a shock to the younger generation leading in many cases to psychological disturbance and split personality. There is also the phenomenon of the spread of narcotics and drugs. Some have become addicted while others have used them for profit.

4 Erroneous concept of the essence of loyalty
Many people of the GCC states originally belong to the same tribes or groups. This identification has in many ways weakened their sense of belonging to the state under whose sovereignty they live in the region. Some have a weak loyalty to the concept expressed in the common regional characteristics of the GCC states. At the same time they are remote from any feeling of national loyalty as Arabs, imagining that this can only be at the expense of other loyalties, or that it conflicts with loyalty to Islam. This has subjected a large section of youth to conflicting pressures which create personality problems and social fragmentation. All of this is due to a mistaken understanding of the meaning of loyalty and of Islamic obligations.

5 Social and cultural alienation
The increasing reliance on foreign manpower among the states of the GCC has resulted in the phenomenon of social and cultural alienation whereby the people of certain regional states have been reduced to no more than a fifth or a sixth of the total population. As the foreigners have become the overwhelming majority, leading the indigenous people

to come to feel strangers in their own land, the social fabric of national unity and cultural identity is threatened. The increase in foreign manpower has changed from a temporary phenomenon to a permanent feature of the economic patter of the Gulf, leading to several negative results such as:

(a) The danger of assigning a secondary role to Arabic in certain Gulf societies which divorces them from their cultural heritage and particularly affects children.

(b) A decline in the activities of women of the Gulf within the family where they have lost or are about to lose the sense of responsibility for bringing up their families as vital elements in society because of the introduction of domestic servants.

(c) The phenomenon of trading in visas and work permits.

(d) Disturbance in the security of society because of an increase in crime such as robbery, burglary, trade in narcotics and crimes of morality.

6 *Maldistribution of national workforce in various kinds of economic activities*
The oil boom created a certain government obligation to employ citizens in various state organs which has led to a form of underemployment in these organs together with a poor quality of performance by the workforce or the lack of certain skills. On the other hand, the distribution of the national workforce according to their professional skills is somewhat faulty because such a large proportion of the workforce tends to concentrate in clerical jobs and the service sector.

7 *Lack of social expertise*
The recently acquired political freedom by the member states of the GCC has been followed by a delay in the creation of different social institutions with a lack of expertise in their administration. Expert leadership cadres capable of bringing about the desired changes in the behaviour pattern of citizens inculcating in them desirable values and concepts and encouraging more advanced patterns of behaviour are not available.

C   National Strategy of GCC States

General

1 In the course of a review of the national aims of the GCC states we have described characteristics of their general policy in the political, military, economic and social fields in the light of what has been incorporated in the charter of the Gulf states and as outlined in the final communiqués of the Higher Council and in the working paper for joint Gulf action. In the second section we have dealt with this working paper and noted the various dangers and risks which confront the GCC states. There is no doubt that a few questions arise from this presentation and these are as follows:

(a) Which path is the most suitable for implementing the general policy of the GCC states?

(b) What is the best possible alternative for facing the dangers and the threats the GCC states are exposed to?

2 The sum total of answers to these two questions is contained in the national strategy of the GCC states and this is what we shall discuss in this section within the framework of the following dimensions: (a) political strategy; (b) economic strategy; (c) social strategy.

Political strategy

1 Strengthening co-ordination and integration among GCC states
(a) The Cooperation Council provides the broad foundation for the GCC states. The establishment of the Council secured for these states a strong defensive wall to repulse hostile ambitions and threats.

(b) The GCC is a symbol of solidarity and a strong edifice not only at the Arab level but also at the international level as has been borne out by regional and international studies conducted about the future of the Arab Gulf. Hence the strengthening of co-ordination and integration between the GCC states in the fields of defence, security, economy and sociology is of vital importance and every step we take in this direction helps to remove the risks and dangers away from the region. Any weakness in the Gulf body politic is an open invitation to disruptive influences among these states whether they come singly or collectively.

2 Adoption of a foreign policy more evenly balanced as between the super-powers

The insulation of the GCC states against international polarization requires the pursuit of a foreign policy which is more balanced as between the two superpowers. We live in a dangerous period of history when the superpowers are fighting a bitter economic struggle. So the opening of an economic window on the eastern camp is bound to have important economic and political implications.

3 Strengthening Arab solidarity and reinforcing the Islamic role

The Arab front is the strategic depth of the GCC states. Therefore the consolidation and strengthening of Arab solidarity in a new way is important and inevitable. A review of the Charter of the Arab League which is the framework for strengthening Arab solidarity, is considered one of the basic subjects which requires a deep study as the earlier experience had certain negative consequences. Once as many as twenty-two states became members of the Arab League it became necessary for decisions to be taken on the basis of majority votes so that there was no scope for one or two states to block progress towards joint Arab action. We believe that the GCC states can play a prominent role in the evolution of the Arab League and in acquiring the required degree of credibility in Arab action. The GCC states have the wider field for strengthening Islamic solidarity by mobilising their potentialities to play a leading role in the Islamic world.

4 Organized confrontation of campaigns of counter-propaganda

This type of confrontation will have to be based on the following:

(a) Mobilization of all information media among the GCC states to confront the counter-propaganda launched against them so that these organs can function within a single framework according to a single programme originating from clear-cut and well defined goals so that there is no confusion or contradiction among them in their methods or initiatives.

(b) Employment of means to promote an internal information campaign among the GCC states which will win the confidence of the citizens and their enthusiastic response to the means adopted.

(c) Providing the information media with the various dimensions of political, economic, social and military planning until it becomes possible for them to understand the various factors involved and lay down media plans in harmony with the goals and general policies of the GCC states.

121

(d) A study of the techniques adopted in counter-propaganda against the GCC states, identification of loopholes which are exploited by the propagandists and the planning of effective measures to combat them.

(e) Consideration of the importance of the role of foreign news agencies with action to help them comprehend the situation prevailing in the region.

Economic strategy

1ᵉ Diversification of sources of income and reduced dependence on oil
Although a considerable period of time has passed since the GCC states became conscious of this problem and in spite of the various pointers to the declining importance of oil, these states have not achieved what they had aspired to. They have continued to depend on oil as the main source of income, thus exposing themselves to crisis situations in the event of a further decline in the importance of oil at the international level. The achievement of this goal requires that the following strategy be followed:

(a) An increase in investments in the productive sectors such as industry, agriculture, fisheries, etc, so that the productive base is widened and a minimum level of self-sufficiency is attained in at least some products.

(b) Placing a ceiling on investments in the trading sector and in import-export activity as it does not play a major role in bringing about basic changes in the economic framework despite its importance. This is due to its linkage with oil, which means that it does not further the aim of achieving diversification in the sources of income and the expansion of the productive base in the economic systems of the GCC states.

(c) Action to achieve stability in the services sector enabling it to play its role in the policy of diversifying the sources of income of the GCC states.

2 Strengthening the industrial sector and making it effective
The GCC states are in urgent need of strengthening the industrial sector and making it effective. This necessitates the following:

A – Drawing an industrial map of the GCC states outlining the extent and size of the industrial sector in all its branches and fixing the scale of the pilot industries which are expected to lead the process of industrial development at the end of the current century or at the beginning of the next century in the light of the anticipated regional and international changes. It is essential that this map should include the following:

1   The nature and type of industrial investments which will provide a substantial inter-linked network of industries in a way that each of them strengthens the other either in terms of inputs or end-product utilization whether partly or entirely at the level of individual countries or at the level of the GCC states as a whole.

2   Established production goals for various local industries in such a way that within a given time-frame 25 per cent of the local products are cycled among the GCC states with importance attached to industries using local primary products especially in agriculture and fisheries.

3   Determination of the amount of financing required to achieve industrial development at the Gulf level and at the level of every individual state of the GCC.

B – Promoting special investment in the industrial sector by deciding on direct facilities such as the allocation of suitable industrial sites at appropriate rates or granting privileges to an industry in utilizing various services linked with domestic consumption or providing indirect facilities such as encouraging the establishment of specialized agencies to study and create opportunities for industrial investments and their financing on easy terms.

C – Conducting an accurate geological survey of the GCC states with the aim of discovering the economic potential of metals and minerals.

D – Adopting the necessary steps to lay down a policy for the transfer, adoption and development of technology for the GCC states as well as a policy for obtaining improved terms through collective bargaining with foreign countries for the transfer of industrial and marketing technology.

E – Unification of industrial legislation and regulations.

3   *Provisions of reserves for future*

Among the important policies which appear necessary in confronting the economic challenge faced by the GCC states is the provision of reserves for future generations. This need grows in importance with the depletion of oil resources or a reduction in their economic potential, particularly as the economic life of the states of the GCC continues to rely heavily on this commodity. It is difficult to envisage continuity in economic activity in these states after the oil resource is depleted or its value reduced. Therefore, before we reach this situation, it is necessary that we preserve our resources in such a way as to guarantee our coming generations a minimum standard of living which will give them confidence and security in their future. Our capacity to create these reserves is made easier by the standard of living enjoyed by the present generation which not only reflects the present stage of development but reaches higher levels of consumption than those of some advanced states and borders on extravagance. It sometimes creates a feeling that we are living not only within our existing resources but also at the expense of coming generations.

4 Redistribution of income and wealth

An important economic policy needed at the level of the GCC states is the adoption of comprehensive steps to achieve the redistribution of income and wealth among citizens in order to reduce the prevailing imbalance. We have explained earlier how this problem of income distribution represents one of the major weaknesses in the social and economic structure of the GCC states. Several studies in which world organizations have participated have repeatedly referred to the importance of meeting this challenge so that a firm foundation of collective security can be laid and the development process is given a clearly collective character which is what the various states of the region are attempting to achieve. In this connection we may refer to certain steps which may help to reduce the gross disparities of income and wealth between individuals and which represent alternatives any one of which may be selected for solving the problem:

(a) The Government in its economic policies may intervene directly to raise the standard of living of those social groups which did not obviously benefit from the new prosperity through continuing its housing policy and increasing subsidies for basic commodities.

(b) Expanding the ownership base in certain successful economic institutions to include the poorer sections of the population as a means of redistribution of income and economic security for a large number of people.

(c) Strengthening the linkage between output and reward in order to reduce the social effects of a wide gap in the distribution of income. When disparities in income result from different levels of performance the resentment they create is much less when there is no apparent relationship between productivity and income. At present we find groups of people who rapidly become very wealthy without justification in the amount they are producing. At the same time we find other groups who in spite of their qualifications and hard work do not receive comparable levels of material rewards. This is not only a form of economic inequity but sometimes appears as a social fraud.

5   *A solution to the phenomenon of economic disparities in income among GCC states*

(a) The question of disparities in income among the states of the GCC in general should also be dealt with at the level of the member states. If we want each state to have similar effectiveness and co-operativeness in carrying out the development plans at the regional level then it is necessary that it should have the same of proportional financial and economic capacity particularly if the principle is conceded that contribution of all the citizens of the Gulf states should be similar. It therefore becomes necessary that they should have comparable levels of the necessary facilities. Otherwise the people will feel that there is a wide disparity in their benefits while their duties and obligations are the same.

(b) The disparities of income among the GCC states have several important consequences far beyond the level of individuals. These often appear in all kinds of activities in varied economic circumstances, and create various obstacles to the progress of integration under the terms of the economic agreement.

6   *Achieving security in food and oil*

The strategic course which must be followed in confronting the economic challenges to which the GCC states are exposed is one of achieving security in food and oil in the event of the region being subjected to internal and external disturbances. Because of the exposed economic situation of the region and its almost total reliance on imports of food and exports of oil, any attempt to isolate the GCC states from the outside world will paralyze their economic life of these states to a dangerous degree. We should consider this seriously and create the necessary safeguards in the following manner:

(a) Arrange buffer stocks of staple food stuffs, lay down the levels of consumption for each state out of these stocks and select suitable sites for their storage. At the same time a reliable distribution network for these stocks should be ensured between the member states.

(b) Oil stocks should be built up on the pattern of food-stocks in such a way that we guarantee the continued provision of this basic need in case of a halt in production. Similarly we need to build up reserve stocks of spare parts needed for oil production and refining which can be used in the event of any breakdown or damage and the time spent in importing them can be saved.

Social strategy

1 Strengthening the domestic fronts in the GCC states
The strategic course needed to achieve this policy objective is as follows:

(a) Preparation of dedicated national cadres and institutions capable of keeping pace with the progress in the social, industrial, scientific, military and administrative fields and in other basic spheres.

(b) Developing and strengthening the security and defence apparatus of each of the GCC states in a co-ordinated and effective manner so that they succeed in containing the disruptive elements who infiltrate into the region and are well-trained in handling political and social conspiracies and terrorism.

(c) Strengthening institutions and agencies which create a positive political consciousness, particularly the official media, in such a way that their role changes from merely being an instrument for reflecting official political positions or merely broadcasting entertainment programmes to becoming effective instruments in creating a positive political consciousness among Gulf citizens and gradually inculcating patriotic conduct in all branches of life.

2 Bringing about desirable social changes for achieving development among GCC states
The strategic course for achieving this policy objective lies in planning and implementing social guidance programmes with the participation of various ministries and other social agencies responsible for information, education, youth and Islamic affairs in order to strengthen the system of values, patterns of behaviour and the nature of social relationships which serve the process of development among the GCC states and bring about changes in a number of values, ingrained behaviour patterns and prevailing relationships which block the development process. This should be done in the following manner:

A – Strengthening the value of participation in the development of society by highlighting the following:

1 The meaning of responsibility arising out of the freedom of the individual and the teachings of his religion in the light of the sayings

of the Holy Prophet, viz, 'Each one of you is a shepherd and each one of you is responsible for his flock', and 'Religion is counsel to the imams of the Muslims and their people.'

2 The meaning of co-operation and 'integration' based on the premise that the opinion of the group is better than that of an individual and hence whatever has been legislated for general good should receive the support of everyone in its administration. This in turn means that the politicians should follow the dictum laid down by God Almighty: 'Help ye one another in righteousness and piety' (S2-V5).

3 Consultation is one of the basic rules of governing in Islam and the necessary concomitant of the virtues of a Muslim who abides by the dictum 'their conduct of affairs is by mutual consultation' (S42-V38). This is a basic pillar of democracy as a contemporary expression of the principle of consultation.

4 Creating a system of incentives and encouragement linked directly or indirectly to the extent of participation in the development of society. Benefit can be derived from the experience of societies which provide for monetary rewards, decorations and certificates of merit for participation in the development of society such as the award of a prize to the outstanding factory worker or school-teacher for service to the community and society, etc. These are different ways of providing the incentives for strengthening the basic value of individual participation as in promoting social action.

B – Strengthening the concept of public service in society by directing attention to the following two sectors:

(i) That of government servants who render various services to the public in its name. These should adopt a change in their approach to those who have dealings with the state by exhibiting an attitude of public service in carrying out their job. Such a role would pave the way for people's participation in the implementation of various projects for development and reform. The creation of training programmes for government servants in norms of behaviour and service will extend the specialized fields of administration entrusted to them.

(ii) The youth sector which should be treated on the basis of a most effective way of inspiring them with a sense of participation in public life does not mean providing them with a wide range of services. Instead they should be asked to contribute to society and the fullest opportunities should be given to them for making their contribution. In this way they will realize their own value and that of playing their part in life. This will be the first stage in realizing their potentials effectively and shielding the community from the consequences of young people plunging into other activities which they think to be their duty but are divorced from the goals of the state.

C – Emphasizing the value of work, production and innovation in the following ways:

(i) Combating the enthusiasm of the youth of the GCC states for highly prestigious work which will give them power over their subordinates and their tendency to belittle manual labour and craftsmanship. The tendency to feel superior to their friends and refuse to perform manual labour can be resisted by invoking the Islamic doctrine of the value of labour and by refusing the recognize the current division of work into prestigious and ordinary jobs.

(ii) Young people should be constantly warned that we have as a nation been overtaken by several centuries of stagnation and sloth while the world around us has progressed by working day and night. We can never catch up with this world merely by increasing our bank balances or importing the products of others with our money, or by employing them to do our work at whatever cost. The only way to catch up with them is for all of us to work together and work hard.

(iii) Strengthening the principle of the virtue of work for the common good as the basis of rendering public service.

(iv) Teaching that the value of work lies not in the number of hours spent on it but on the added value it creates. Society should work in order to produce, otherwise work can be as unproductive as ploughing the sea – a useless expenditure of energy. Society does not progress as a result. We should also combat the notion prevalent among many individuals and workers of the GCC states that respect for official working hours is the only measure of value. It should be made clear that ultimately what matters in work is that society sees its value in terms of results.

(v) It should be stated that real progress is never achieved except through innovation and initiative marked by improved performance. The record of scientific and technological revolutions achieved by certain highly advanced nations shows that it is due to their initiative and superior performance. Our future will be tragic if we convince ourselves that we have the least need to work and produce and can be satisfied with a poor imitation of others without tackling the unknown or achieving expertize in what is known merely by repetition. We should emphasize the value of innovation in addition to laying down rules for encouraging merit an rewarding those who produce practical and theoretical ideas both within the country and at the Gulf level.

(vi) A commitment to achieving justice should be emphasized in the organization of labour relations. If justice is contravened in one way or another, it will damage the work itself and in turn lead to the creation of social tension and deteriorating human relationships threatening the fabric of social peace. If legislation were to lay down the limits of rights and obligations in labour relations, then the responsible organs of stage should endeavour to implement these rules and regulations to solve the disputes which may arise in a spirit of justice, objectivity and human equality. This is essential in ensuring stability, social peace and workers' enthusiasm for their work. It should constantly be recalled that it is necessary to consolidate labour relations on the basis of a balance between rights and duties where 'no one oppresses or is oppressed'.

D – Guidance as to the value of time.

This is meant by highlighting what the societies of the GCC states have achieved by their contact with the outside world and the ways in which life has been orientated towards industry by the process of industrialization. In spite of the relative spread of education and culture there is an insufficient appreciation among many citizens of the meaning of time.

They do not seem to attach much importance to time-frames in their lives. It is necessary to warn them of the need to keep within time-scales and perform both large and small tasks within the times laid down for their implementation according to the highest standard.

E – Instillation of respect for rules and regulations.

This is achieved through general participation in their determinations so that they are not totally alien to or beyond the comprehension of those to whom they apply or are not contrary to their aims and interests. It is important to observe the application of various rules and regulations and gauge their public acceptance as just, appropriate and of equitable application to all irrespective of their social standing or official status. This strengthens the framework of justice, the concept of state and authority and the requirements of security and social stability in accordance with the saying of the Holy Prophet: 'Those who came before you were destroyed because if any one of them from among the nobles committed theft they left him alone, but if a weak one among them committed theft, then they were given the punishment laid down.'

In addition the basic rules should be clearly defined and the citizens should be educated about their rights and obligations based on these rules and regulations.

F – Activization of women's role in social life.

This is done by emphasizing the basic principles of the Islamic concept of women which laid down the rights of women and recognized their independent legal personality and their rights to property distinct from men's rights. It is necessary that the policies of social change should devote a greater measure of attention to women and the activization of their role in society whether it is related to looking after the husband or the upbringing of children or to whatever concerns their participation in all parts of the developmental plans in every sense.

G – Dealing with the phenomenon of dependence on the past and Westernization of culture.

The rapid modern awakening and the adoption of different facets of Western culture marked by materialism have led to a polarization in thought between a denial of this culture and reversion to the past with a bigoted outlook and rejecting the past altogether and abandoning its values and beliefs. What is needed is a modern thought process which will preserve the values of our heritage while drawing from western culture what is needed to become familiar with the realities of the present without damage to the basic ideals of faith and the spiritual life.

H – Resistance to consumerism and setting a limit to expenditure.

This is done by concentrating on the value of balance in expenditure and conserving what is purchased. Only what is essential should be bought and the scale of luxury items should not be extended. It must be said that the phenomenon of ever-increasing consumerism has reached such an extent in the societies of the GCC states that they have accepted it as a way of life which imposes on these states an unacceptable and unjustified burden. This threatens the various service facilities of the state, such as the production of electricity and the provision of water, etc. with breakdown. It also threatens public health because of diseases resulting from extravagance in the consumption of food which can be considered a great danger to the capacity of the new generation to bear the burdens and challenges of life.

3 Dealing with the problem of identification with country, region and nation
This means concentrating on the importance of liberating the concept of nationalism from misconceptions such as considering the Arab race as superior and enjoying a right of sovereignty because of its pure racial extraction. There is no doubt that the racial concept is totally repugnant to Islam which declares the brotherhood of all believers and affirms that 'an Arab has no preference over a non-Arab nor a non-Arab over an Arab except in piety'. There is a need also to liberate the concept of nationalism from regarding Islam merely as one movement of Arab awakening in a succession of Arab movements. This leads to attempts to construct contemporary Arab societies divorced from Islam although it is abundantly clear that such an idea is a pure exercise in futility. The contemporary Arab has no civilizational and cultural heritage apart from Islam and Islam with its culture and values is subjectively and historically the mainstay of Arab life. Similarly, some prevalent views of Islam should be purged of misconceptions about the meaning of nationalism. There is nothing in Islam to prevent it from moving politically towards national unification. This will put an end to ideological and psychological divisions arising from an illogical conflict between nationalist imperatives and Islamic obligations. The effect of such fragmentation will not be confined to the lives of individual citizens of the GCC states but will also extend to Gulf societies as a whole as the various political, cultural and social divisions among them damage and weaken them and destabilize them politically.

4 Organizing employment of the expatriate workforce and dealing with its effects
The strategy direction for achieving this objective is as follows:

(a) Laying down a joint programme at the level of the GCC states for a phased reduction in the number of foreigners who were brought in during a period of economic reconstruction and who mainly came to participate in the creation of basic public utilities. Now that these have been largely completed and with the slowing-down in the pace of economic development compared with previous years, it is natural that the need for foreign labour should decline particularly when increasing numbers of the indigenous population are entering the employment market every year.

(b) To work for a return to our Arab Islamic roots in Gulf societies and encourage them to revert to Arabic in the conduct of daily life.

5   Developing Gulf manpower and its balanced distribution according to types of economic activities
The necessary strategy for realizing this policy is represented by the following:

(a) Assessment of the facilities for training available in the GCC states in terms of their specialization, standards and location together with the periods of training and equipment and the training offered both in terms of quantity and quality.

(b) Laying down the training needs within a future time-frame both at the level of each state and that of the GCC states as a whole.

(c) A comparative appraisal of the training potentials and needs, deciding the extent of what is lacking and exploring potentials which have remained untapped, if such exist.

(d) Preparing a training plan covering all the GCC states in all sectors and for all types of training.

(e) Concentrating in the training programme on providing a certain number of Gulf workers with the necessary skills and qualifications to enable local talent to replace the foreign workforce particularly in those strategic positions concerned with production, services, the higher levels of administration, senior executives in various departments, the scientific and technical professions and supervision of the labour force.

(f) Raising the level of participation of women among the GCC states in the workforce.

(g) Retaining employees of the government sector in the GCC states to deal effectively with the phenomenon of unemployment.

Summary of strategies – political, economic and social

1   Political strategy

(a)   Strengthening co-ordination and integration among the GCC states.
(b)   Following a more balanced foreign policy between the super-powers.
(c)   Working to strengthen Arab solidarity and making the necessary amendments to the Charter of the League of Arab states to intro-duce the principle of majority decisions.
(d)   Organizing responses to hostile propaganda campaigns.

2 *Economic strategy*

(a) Diversification of the sources of income and a progressive reduction in the total reliance on oil.
(b) Strengthening the industrial sector and making it effective.
(c) Provision of reserves for future generations.
(d) Revision of the distribution of income and wealth.
(e) Dealing with the effects of wide disparities in wealth and income among the GCC states.
(f) Achieving food and oil security.

3 *Social strategy*

(a) Strengthening the internal fronts within the GCC states.
(b) Bringing about desirable social development through means adjusted to the programme of development in the GCC states as follows:
    (i)   Strengthening the value of individual participation in the development of society.
    (ii) Strengthening the concept of public service in society.
    (iii) Emphasizing the value of work, production and innovation.
    (iv) Stressing the value of time.
    (v)   Preparing women to perform their role in social life.
    (vi) Rectifying the phenomena either of clinging to the past or adopting a Westernized culture.
    (vii) Resisting unbridled consumerism and limiting obstentatious expenditure.
(c) Rectifying faulty concepts of identity on the basis of country, region and nation.
(d) Organizing the employment of foreign manpower and taking measure to rectify its effects.
(e) Developing the workforce of the Gulf and achieving its balanced distribution between different types of economic activity.
(f) Providing training to create skills and expertise.

D The Concept of Military Strategy of the GCC states

The military threat

General
(a) This region, over the passage of centuries, has been the centre of attention of big powers because of its strategic position at the crossroads

of three continents. The ambitions of the various powers towards this region have increased enormously over the last five decades because of the discovery of oil and the consequent high level of its wealth. The position was not so clear-cut during the days of British protection in some of the GCC states because of a tacit understanding between the big powers that this region was in the Western zone of influence. But the withdrawal of Britain from the region created a different situation which was referred to by the big powers as a power vacuum. Each of these powers tried to bring some or all the states of this region under their direct political influence and subject them to their control. This constituted a direct threat to their security and safety as they stood in the crossfire between the competing powers in the region.

(b) From the outset there was increasing hatred for Islam which is the nation's religion, the basic of its civilization and cultural heritage. This was apparent in the Mongol and Tartar invasions, the Crusades and the colonial invasions which continued until present times with the aim of weakening the Muslims and subduing them. This led to an Arab and Islamic reaction which played a major role in ejecting the occupation forces from the various parts of this region.

(c) When the colonial powers were unable to achieve all their aims in liquidating Arab values and Islam, they adopted a new technique of creating a forward base from which they could launch their aggression against our land and thus Israel came to implement their plans by striking at the Arab nation and shattering its potential. Our region in the Gulf is no longer insulated from the ambitions of Israel.

(d) Political developments in the region in the years since 1979 have revealed a kind of destructive conspiracy against the GCC states to subvert their internal structure and encourage sectarianism and division among the people of a single nation.

The aim
The aim of this study is to analyse the threats which emanate from our enemies.

Proof of the threat
The threat is contained in the instigation of the people of this region, the training of some of them as saboteurs and their despatch to carry out acts of sabotage inside the GCC states by blowing up vital installations and smuggling in weapons.

Summary of military threats

The foreign threats to the GCC states and continued conspiracies against them require the implementation of a joint defence agreement and the removal of differences between the member states. This alone can thwart all types of threat against them.

Essential elements of military strategy to face foreign threats

1 Developing the armed forces in the GCC states.
2 Laying down a defence plan and creating a unified command to face the encircling dangers which threaten the Gulf states.
3 Protection of the naval and air routes of the Gulf region.
4 Protection of vital installations in the Gulf states.
5 Warding off the enemy and destroying him if he commits aggression.

Joint action

Joint military action by the GCC states should be planned with emphasis on the raising of forces and their effective use for achieving the country's and the nation's goals. Therefore the military concept of the GCC states should, generally speaking, be based on twin responsibilities which are: Raising of forces and planning of operations for the short, medium and long term. In other words, joint military action by the Gulf states should proceed from a planned appreciation of the needs for raising and employing military forces and preparing them for future as well as immediate confrontations. In this matter joint action should concentrate on achieving deterrence through the possession of an adequate force.

General bases for collective defence

Military co-operation for the collective defence of the Gulf states derives from the religious, national and historical ties which bind them. Their common characteristics and similarities unify them culturally, economically and socially in addition to the brotherly relations which bind them. They have a common aim to fulfil and a common destiny awaits them. In order to strengthen this co-operation and improve its effectiveness, it is essential that the following points be taken into consideration:

• Raising of forces by the GCC states themselves.
• 'Al-Jazira (Peninsula) Shield' forces.
• Supporting reserve forces.
• Maintenance.
• General mobilization and civil defence.

A   Raising of forces by the GCC states

It is necessary to constitute the armed forces of the GCC states in a coordinated manner first by building up those of the individual states as well as collectively. They should utilize all the potentials and resources which are available in this connection in the context of the strategy of joint defence as outlined in paragraph 6 of the decisions of the Conference of Defence Ministers which was held in Riyadh on 25 January 1982. The conference discussed the recommendations for the raising of armed forces in member states individually within the ambit of the overall concept. This concept was agreed by everyone after taking into consideration the need to avoid duplication and ensure integration. This imposes on us the following tasks:

1   Drawing the geographical boundaries of the theatre of operations for the land forces as well as for naval and air operations. This should be announced openly and clearly.

2   Continuation of joint training among the armed forces of the Gulf states with defined goals.

3   Creating a unified air defence system strengthened by interceptor aircraft operating under a joint air defence command to achieve air supremacy. The nature of this task will require constant readiness and tracking for the detection and destruction of hostile air targets round the clock.

4   Organizing visits and field reconnaissances by commanders and officers of the armed forces of the GCC states to various theatres of operations so that they can familiarize themselves with the geography of the area and its sea and air defence needs.

5   Laying down a clear policy for the military expenditure involved in programmes for equipping and arming the armed forces of the GCC states. There should also be a clear agreement over the financial outlay involved in joint military studies for promoting joint Gulf action under the close supervision of the General Secretariat of the GCC states.

6   Promoting the work of the military committee which has played an effective role in achieving military coordination between the armed forces of the GCC states. This would best serve the policy of joint action during the coming period by conducting studies and planning for coordination and integration and working for laying down a general defence plan based on comprehensive field studies which take into account all eventualities and the available forces with the GCC states for facing external threats. This will guarantee coordination between the

armed forces of the GCC states in the fields of training, equipment, weaponry and their levels of preparedness.

7 Continuance of cooperation with Arab and Islamic armies to achieve strategic and manpower depth for the forces of the GCC states.

B Forces of the 'Peninsula Shield'

1 Aim
While the responsibility for the security of the Gulf rests with its own people, each Gulf state is not individually strong enough. On the basis of the faith of the leaders of the GCC states in the unity of their goal, and common destiny and their desire to achieve coordination, liaison and integration which will ultimately lead to a comprehensive unity, it was agreed that the 'Peninsula Shield' force should be constituted by the Gulf states. This was to be the first stage in the unification of military efforts among these states to ensure the defence and stability of the region in the light of the joint defence plan aimed at foiling the attempts of the various competing powers to gain control over this region.

2 Development of the forces of 'Peninsula Shield'
(a) The situation prevailing in the region during the year 1981 necessitated the formation of the Peninsula Shield by the GCC states for the purpose of immediately intervening if any state was subjected to aggression. These forces conducted training exercise 'Peninsula Shield' in the United Arab Emirates and the Kingdom of Saudi Arabia as part of a joint training plan which achieved a resounding success at the level of the Gulf and other states.

(b) The Peninsula Shield forces are intended to absorb the first shock in confronting any enemy which may threaten one of the GCC states. For these forces to play their role competently it is necessary for them to be developed and in the following ways:

(i)   Their size and composition.
(ii) Their weaponry and fire support.
(iii) Training that is realistic in relation to likely threats.
(iv) High standard of combat-readiness in order to reach the state most exposed to threat before it develops.

C   *Reserve support forces*

1   *Reserve forces*

The role of the armed forces in the GCC states should be to give real support to the Peninsula Shield in such a way that they become the general reserve of the Peninsula Forces which are contributed by each state. The big question that remains is how it would be possible to implement the principle of reserve forces to support the Peninsula Forces. The Bahrain Defence Force considers it absolutely necessary for the support forces to be trained to a higher level of military capability and fighting potential in case the Peninsula Shield is left to its own devices. Hence it is necessary to develop the armies of the GCC states and modernize their weapons in order for them to be able to carry out their responsibilities to the full. It may be appropriate to apply the principle of the division of various roles between them until such time as the GCC states complete their own build-up.

2   *Distribution of roles*

Distribution of roles means that a state which has a good military potential should exploit it in the service of the other Gulf states which may be deficient in that respect. This support should continue until the build-up in those states is completed.

D   *Maintenance*

There are international standards for the maintenance needs of forces, weapons and equipment. In view of the great importance attached to maintenance and its close linkage with the development and modernization of military institutions and the great effect it has on the conduct of battle, it is necessary to lay down a comprehensive programme for the maintenance of the forces of the GCC states by taking into account the following basic factors:

1   A unified system of maintenance and supplies.
2   Concentration and storage of supplies in the likely theatres of operation.
3   Unification of the weapons system to the maximum to reduce the load on maintenance.
4   Laying down of realistic plan for providing administrative support and for training in these methods.
5   Flexibility of organization for systems of administrative support.

6 Laying down of standing orders for logistical support in peace and war.
7 A move towards establishing some of the military industries in the GCC states to reduce total dependence on external sources.
8 Creating advanced maintenances centres.

E   *General mobilization and civil defence*

The question of general mobilization comes within the framework of general preparation for war by the state. In this respect it is necessary that the following points are taken into consideration by the GCC states as soon as possible in order to ensure strong support for the armed forces of the GCC states:

1   *General mobilization*

(a) Creating a system of reserves in the armed forces.
(b) Co-ordination with other government ministries with regard to general mobilization.
(c) Maintenance of strategic reserves at the state level to include all consumer goods.
(d) Laying down a plan for mobilizing all the resources of the state for defence.
(e) Laying down plans for the defence of vital installations with the greatest importance to the country.

2   *Civil defence*

(a) Creating an integrated system for civil defence.
(b) Preparing the various sectors of national civil defence and the mobilization of all potentials and resources for battle.
(c) Preparing shelters to have them ready for use by the citizens during military operations.

3   *Psychological preparedness*

(a) Laying down of plans for confronting hostile psychological warfare.
(b) Using all information media in the service of national goals.
(c) Co-ordination of information among the GCC states to promote the basic goals of the Council.
(d) Prepare the citizens of the GCC states psychologically.

Summary of joint action
The possibility of aggression makes planning and joint action among the GCC states a vitality for confronting such hostile action. This requires the following:

(i) Agreement over a studied plan for developing the armed forces of the GCC states.
(ii) Developing self-reliance of these forces with all possible speed.
(iii) Strengthening the general military position of the GCC states and coordination of their efforts to achieve this goal. This would involve different kinds of individual action which should be coordinated so as to lead to group action and joint training exercises. The following should be taken into consideration in this regard:

(a) The adoption of weapon systems which are capable of meeting any potential threat.
(b) Strengthening of training programmes in general.
(c) Emphasis on specialist training.

4 *Laying down a comprehensive defence plan*
For the GCC states to achieve the following goals:

(a) Protection of the naval and air routes of the region.
(b) Protection of the vital installations of the GCC states against sabotage (special operations).
(c) Deterring and destroying the enemy if he commits aggression against any of the GCC states.

5 *A system of command and control*
For co-ordinating the general effort of the forces of the GCC states and for decision-making in the light of information which reaches the general command.

Arab and Islamic Dimensions

1 *Arab dimension*
Bahrain considers it essential to look at the Arab world as representing strategic depth for the GCC states politically, geographically and in terms of manpower. This arises out of their religious, national and historical ties which bind them to a common destiny and make them a political and military force of great consequence in this part of the world.

2 Islamic dimension

The moderate and constructive values of the Islamic faith, the concept 'holy struggle' in its original sense of just war in self-defence, and the patterns of Islamic social action are in Bahrain's view the basic factors in creating integrated systems to reinforce any kind of strategy whether political, military, economic, social or psychological. The call if Islam is based on a clear principle advocating mutual support and cooperation among Muslims. The struggle is a vital necessity for protecting the state's resources and strengthening the security and stability of the people of the region; it is not for aggression but to repel it. From this it becomes clear that we should strengthen the pillars of faith so that it becomes the mainspring for modern thought in the development of a military potential and the drive for economic progress in the building-up of Islamic societies. Such a strategy means an intensification of Islamic action which is the best way to confront the challenges posed by foreign ambitions.

Summary

---

1 Strategic Concept of the GCC States

What has been stated about this concept in the form of a few brief points is only to emphasise what has been said earlier. This matter was discussed by the various defence ministers of the GCC states with the aim of strengthening the basis for joint military action. The very existence of a bold and clear strategy of the GCC states guarantees the continuity of this admirable process and simplifies a great many issues connected with the GCC states. The seventh recommendation of the Chiefs of Staff was ratified by the Ministers of Defence at their meeting held in Riyadh on 25 January 1982 when they stated that: 'The conference studied in detail the seventh recommendation about laying down the strategic concept of the joint defence of the GCC states and decided to entrust the chiefs of staff with the task of conducting studies of the proposal to ensure the development of a plan.'

Our strategy for the GCC states concentrates basically on a policy of deterrence against any aggressor through the implementation of a joint defence plan, a study of our real defence capabilities and of our political, economic, social and military potentials so that we may determine the level of military engagement in the light of these facts. We should rely on raising the armed forces in each state in the light of our goals and roles which are clear and interlinked between all the states of the GCC. This will ensure economy of effort and expenditure in achieving deterrence and confronting and destroying the hostile forces by implementing the principle of distribution of roles in the near future.

2 Defence Plan

The strategic importance of the Gulf region makes it imperative for the GCC states to formulate comprehensive and complementary defence plans to face the dangers of confronting them while totally rejecting those big powers who claim imaginary responsibilities for the defence and security of this region. The defence plan of the future should be comprehensive and integrated and should concentrate on strengthening the principle of the will to fight among the armed forces of the GCC states. This must be tied to political decisions and a clear method of dealing with any potential danger based on the assumptions derived from studies of a general strategic concept. In addition there should be reliance on the Peninsula Shield Forces constituted by the GCC states as a nucleus to be developed as a force for joint action within the framework of the defence plan of the GCC states and to be strengthened by the provision of the necessary support weapons. This will give it a greater effectiveness in deterring any enemy before he thinks in terms of invading one of the Gulf states. The principle of cooperating with our brothers and friends outside the GCC states should also be taken into consideration.

Conclusion

1 The political, military, economic and social dimensions of the national strategy of the GCC states are fully interlinked and integrated. Any weakness in any link in the chain will naturally lead to the weakening of the other links and render it ineffective. Similarly, the effectiveness of these dimensions in achieving the national goals of the GCC states, are primarily dependent on deterrent military power.

2 The success of the GCC states in realizing their aims is heavily dependent on exploiting the close cohesion between Gulf societies, and their identities, and traditions and their capacity to build bridges between the past and the present in working out a general policy which takes into consideration the political, military, economic and social dimensions. This should be followed by the determination of a strategy which will point to the best way of implementing that policy. Thereafter, the aims and priorities of this general policy will have to be converted into specific programmes and projects. They must be provided with the means for their implementation. The process of implementation will have to be reviewed and evaluated periodically.

3 It appears that the attention paid to the strategic framework in the coming phase will provide a basic guarantee for the realisation of the goals of the GCC states to ensure all actions are realistic and based on sound decisions.

4 In the course of this study summarizing our philosophy of defence we shall, God willing, progress along the right path towards collective action by our different states. This will require us to make sound decisions and implement them. The 'First Light' is but the beginning of our march on the true path.

Epilogue

I believe that the reader will have noticed that the main chapters of this book revolved around the military history of Bahrain, both ancient and modern, together with contemporary concerns and visions of the future co-operation between Bahrain and the fellow members of the Gulf Co-operation Council.

The source of my interest in Bahrain's military past, present and future has always been my personal experience and the responsibility of leadership in Bahrain's Defence Force since its establishment. This concern has been the daily fare which I have shared with the officers and soldiers of that force. We work together to develop it into an effective force of its kind based on quality not quantity, according to the policy and principles followed in all the national development fields in Bahrain since its recent renaissance, which seeks qualitative achievement first and foremost. I trust that the reader has noticed, also, the degree of inter-connection between the political, economic, social and cultural fields on the one hand the military field on the other, so that these chapters, in the final analysis, represent a comprehensive review of the Bahraini experience in all these aspects.

I consider this book, in a way, a tale of a small and distinct country and an account of its struggle for self-preservation, continued development and progress despite all the challenges it faces in this sensitive corner of the world.

The 'Bahraini example' provides a living proof that a small productive country can become an important factor in the stability and development of the region in which it exists, and thereafter in the entire world provided that it knows how to organize and manage its domestic affairs with wisdom and efficiency setting a good example to its neighbours, and provided also it knows, with the same degree of awareness, how to deal with these neighbours, the other major powers of the world, and all the members of the international community. Bahrain's relations with its neighbours and the rest of the world are based on mutual understanding, positive co-operation and sincerity, and adherence to observing the principles of reliability and trustworthiness – the very characteristics which were upheld by generations of Bahraini leaders in dealing with their friends under all circumstances, as those friends know full well.

What makes us go back to the true beginning of renaissance and progress in the Gulf area is that many of the writings about the area, whether Arab or Western, focus on the current features with regard to finance, construction and consumption, and do not seek out the deep roots of real progress in this area. If these studies had tried to comprehend the true nature of these roots, they would have discovered that it has been the cultural soil of Bahrain which has attracted, nourished and nurtured them since the dawn of the modern area. The tree of progress grew gradually until its branches covered the entire Gulf area, to the benefit of all Bahrain's brothers in the Gulf.

For the benefit of readers from outside the region, we should mention, briefly, a few of the factors which link the past of this sensitive region with its present.

Historical studies have revealed that the modern systems of commerce, economy, management and government started in Bahrain in the closing decades of the nineteenth century and then spread gradually to the rest of the region in the twentieth century. Bahrain witnessed, also, the modern education movement which was related to enlightenment, renaissance and progress; it then penetrated the other societies and peoples in the region. It is hard to find an intellectual in the Gulf area who is not connected in some way, with the cultural or educational movement in Bahrain. Bahrain was the bridgehead for the teams of oil explorers who then travelled to the northern and southern regions of the Gulf and into the depths of Arabia. The well organized and open social, commercial, and political environment in Bahrain, created a suitable climate for oil exploration in those difficult times in this part of the world. This helped the achievements of exploration which were followed by the first industrial installations necessary for the greatest economic discovery and the setting up of the biggest energy industry in the world in modern times – the oil industry of the Gulf and Arabia. It is the industry which became the lifeline for the world economy, the major industrial powers and the international community in general.

The recent Gulf War (1990–1) showed the extent to which the world understands this reality and its readiness to defend it, when it is endangered, through an international coalition unprecedented in modern history. Due to its central position in the Gulf, Bahrain provided the vital link.

Since the discovery of oil, Bahrain has remained the primary base for the region's communications with the world by sea and air and now through satellites. It has also become the pivotal point for TV transmissions from West and East.

Bahrain also plays host to many foreign banks and international investment offices, which makes it one of the most important financial centres in the world, situated between New York and London in the West and Singapore, Hong Kong and Tokyo in the East.

This was not a 'mutation' in Bahrain's history. Behind it there lies 5000 years of continuous civilization. The process started when Bahrain was the centre of the Dilmun civilization which existed alongside that of the Babylonians, Sumerians and ancient Egyptians, in the cradle of civilization which was in the Near East before the classical European civilizations of Greece, Rome and Byzantium.

The world centres of historical and archaeological studies which follow the continuing historical and archaeological discoveries in this archipelago of over 33 islands, realize the significance of the Sumerian dictum 'Let Dilmun [ancient Bahrain] be the Port of the World'.

The government and people of Bahrain do not invoke these facts as mere historic memories or stories from the past to be repeated with pride. We still live with these facts in the ways of the modern age. We are determined to continue to exploit and develop them as an integral part of the new renaissance in our country and the other Gulf states.

With its pioneering role, Bahrain presents – according to expert opinion – an early model of the 'Post-Oil' age in the Gulf. It does that by attempting to expand, and diversify its economic base depending on its highly developed services and the well-qualified Bahraini human resources. This is the question of the future and a responsibility which had to be faced in this area, regardless of the size of our oil reserves. For oil is, as we all know, an unrenewable resource.

I invite all the pessimists about the future of the Gulf area in the post-oil era to come and study the Bahraini preparations for this eventuality. They may discover the possibilities of developing the economy, society and ideas in order to live in any age and adapt oneself to it without relying entirely on one commodity.

Ironically, Bahrain represents today the first 'post-oil model' in the Gulf, as it did in the 1930s when it became the first 'oil-age model'. Bahrain's experience influenced the area and led the other Arab countries in the Gulf to focus their development strategies on diversifying their economic bases and moving away from relying totally on one commodity, however important that commodity might be.

The reader may also have noticed, by following the events witnessed by Bahrain and the Gulf throughout modern and ancient history, that the region has always been poised between the factors of stability and development on the one hand and those of challenge and turmoil on the other. Although the area occupies an important strategic and economic position, the many powers and conflicting groups around the Gulf, dictated the need for foresight, wisdom, patience, co-operativeness and quiet diplomacy to achieve the right strategic balance to ensure stability and progress. This is a concern which is high on the agenda of all leaders – in the Gulf, in the Arab countries and the rest of the world – in their efforts to enhance the new state of stability which arose from supporting the commitments of 'international legitimacy' in the entire region after the latest Gulf War.

When the first edition of this book appeared in Arabic in 1986, the first Gulf War between Iraq and Iran was still raging after six years. Two years after its end, the region experienced another crisis, which led to a second war that was much wider in its regional and international consequences. Thus the area witnessed two major wars during one decade. That is not a minor occurrence in the life of states and peoples and it has a major effect on their armies. The military developments which occurred after the book was published might justify expanding the chapters dealing with military history and focusing on its various aspects, in order to provide a better assessment of the kind of challenges faced in this sensitive region throughout its entire history.

No matter how new the latest developments may be, they do not represent a complete break with the past, and we must absorb the lessons of history to face the present and the future in a better way. If some people do not believe that history can repeat itself, they must agree, at least, that it contains a number of basic laws and phenomena which recur and repeat their effects in the present, as they did in the past in one way or another.

If all the human will, in its wise and rational form, is to play any role in directing events, then we are required – peoples and leaders in the region and all those in the international community concerned with its affairs as partners in stability and progress – to show a better understanding of the characteristics of the region, in order to achieve the right balance to provide it with stability and well-being, for the good of the peoples of the region and the world at large especially now when the entire Middle East is launched on a practical peace project aimed at ending the longest and most bitter conflict in the modern history of the region, i.e. the Arab-Israeli conflict.

However, peace cannot be achieved in one part of a region and be left exposed to new threats elsewhere in that region. Comprehensive peace is not divisible, and we should work towards enhancing it everywhere at the same time, here in the Gulf and in the Arab East. Everyone remembers only too well how the second Gulf War entailed the risk of a new Arab-Israeli war when missiles were launched southwards and westwards indiscriminately. Modern warfare does not allow peace to be achieved in one part of the region and not in the other; the euphoria of peace between the Arabs and the Israelis must not distract us from maintaining the conditions of stability, or continuing peace, in a sensitive area such as the Gulf in which the world had spent enormous efforts at colossal cost to re-establish the strategic and military balance.

In our judgement, the first condition for maintaining the balance is to try to reduce the regional tension which is rising again, and is taking the shape of renewed territorial claims between certain neighbouring countries.

It will be a great mistake for those concerned with the future peace and stability of the area to view these border disputes as bilateral matters concerning only the parties to the dispute, and to leave it at that without taking clear and decisive position as to who is at fault and where the truth lies.

The experiences of recent political history in the Gulf have shown that the most dangerous armed conflicts were started by territorial claims, border disputes and the breaching of recognized frontiers.

The first Gulf War started with territorial claims in the Shatt al-Arab and other border areas, coupled with each side's attempt to change the recognized and existing borders.

The sudden crisis which led to the second Gulf War started with Iraq's claims to islands, waters, territories and oilfields belonging to Kuwait.

Some countries in the region showed wisdom and flexibility and goodwill, which enabled them to reach acceptable settlements and border demarcations based on mutual understanding, fairness and justice, and these were welcomed regionally and internationally. But that is not always the case, where claims to waters and land are not restricted to borderlines but extend to affect the territorial integrity of a neighbouring country which has been observing recognized frontiers. Cases like these are the starting-point of aggression against the neighbour's territorial integrity and security. Worse still, in some cases these claims have been accompanied by the actual use of force in some way to alter the internationally recognized status quo. This may lead to military conflicts which are not confined to the immediate area under dispute. That, in turn, could lead this sensitive area of the world into a series of regional wars. Any border dispute can drag into it more than one regional power, and thus risk the start of a major war.

The forces of international legitimacy which worked hard to restore security and stability to the Gulf by liberating Kuwait, are asked not to waste the fruits of those gigantic efforts by ignoring the existence of the same kind of sparks which turned into the flames of the last two wars in one decade. I refer to the sparks of the territorial claims which look at first like side issues that can be ignored as border issues between brothers and neighbours, but soon become real causes for dangerous aggression, occupation and war on both regional and global scales.

Instead of having to face a large fire after it has spread, it is wiser to extinguish the small sparks which can cause it. Thus, the first step to secure the state of international legitimacy in the region should be the recognition of existing borders which have been known to exist since independence. However, if the files of territorial claims between the neighbouring countries – historical, geographical and demographic – were to be reopened, then the entire map of the region would have to be redrawn. The results will be of not benefit to those who claimed territory from the other in the first place!

The simple and clear principle of regarding existing and known borders as legitimate and recognized as such, should be adopted in the Gulf region, as it has been upheld by regional and international consensus in many regions – as was the case with the Organization of African Unity, for example. This principle will be an important guarantee of peace and security in our region. If we are to remain optimistic about peace and stability in the entire world in order to enhance the credibility of the new world order, as it is called in the vocabulary of international politics, then we hope that the countries of this region will reach this mutual understanding, based on the principles of international legitimacy, and covered by international guarantees, similar to other collective security arrangements in the world. Such an arrangement is consistent with the situation in the civilized word, and could be the basis for development and the fulfilment of the aspirations of the peoples in the region, for prosperity and dignified existence. It would replace the wasted efforts and military spending required for the futile confrontations and baseless claims, which result in nothing but destruction and suffering for all, as has been demonstrated in the history of all wars. We hope we have seen the last of all wars here in the Gulf and the Middle East, and in the entire world. If this is achieved and stability reigns, the battle for comprehensive development will begin. It will not be easier than military battles, and will require greater abilities of leadership, management and planning, in development and construction.

While man can destroy what he dislikes in days through war the test of development requires him to prove his ability to build gradually over decades.

The oil-producing Gulf states have always faced demands from other countries for their participation in the funding of development projects in many parts of the world. These demands are being renewed today as the Middle East begins a new era.

The oil states in the Gulf never hesitated to assist in various development projects in Arab, Muslim and other countries. We are confident that their participation in the new comprehensive development projects in the Middle East will receive the proper attention of the Gulf leaders, provided that a just and comprehensive peace does materialize.

However, everyone should realize that the oil states of the Gulf face crucial responsibilities regarding the progress of development in their own societies. They have to maintain infrastructure projects and other manufacturing and service industries established in the previous stage, in addition to attempting to answer the growing aspirations of their citizens who are increasing in numbers.

Moreover, the Gulf states are not equal in wealth and vary in their oil production, as is shown among the members of the Gulf Cooperation Council. It is logical to expect the richer members of the Council to help the other members to meet the needs of their development projects. This will ensure a more equal level of prosperity and income among the states and their individual citizens and guarantee stability and prosperity for all of them.

It is not logical to ask the oil states of the Gulf to contribute heavily towards development programmes outside the region, while the Cooperation Council states suffer from disparities in national and individual incomes and are at different levels of development.

If this matter is not addressed, it can become a destabilizing factor, socially, economically and psychologically for the general public, within the overall structure of the Council in the medium and long terms. It may also have a negative effect on security and political stability in general. These are matters which the Council tries to deal with and contain.

The experience of modern history, throughout the world, proves that stability and prosperity are essential and indivisible. If they are not enjoyed by everyone then everyone will be at risk. This is well demonstrated by the European Community's efforts at all levels to close the gaps in economic and living standards among its member states.

Finally, if this book opened with a word about the beginnings of Bahrain as a country, state and an experience, it is only fitting also to end with a word about Bahrain.

Bahrain is the only country in the Arab world which is an archipelago consisting of over 33 islands in an organically related marine system. It is the only country in the world to have a name derived from 'sea'. The word 'Bahrain' means in Arabic 'Two Seas', i.e. the salt waters surrounding the islands and fresh water from marine springs close to the small islands and other springs on dry land. These springs have been the source of life for its citizens: sailors, divers and fishermen. The sea waters were the source of their food: sea-food and fish.

The sea is essential to Bahrain. The country gained an historic reputation for producing natural pearls and for the maritime trade through the ages associated with it. Bahrain's seafaring activities reached out to the entire world and interacted with its people and cultures.

This characterizes Bahrain as a true maritime country, in contrast to other Arab countries, despite the fact that they may have coastlines.

It is an essential ingredient of Bahrain's tradition, both popular and cultural, which is characterized by openness and tolerance towards other people, acceptance of useful new ideas and achievements and moderation in all attitudes, policies and public and private behaviour. It is combined with the fundamentals of Bahrain's national identity; an Arab and Muslim identity through which it shares its nationality with the Arab world and with the Islamic culture – its creed and spiritual and human values.

In conclusion, I find nothing which could better illustrate the Bahraini fundamentals than when I wrote in chapter 3 of this book entitled 'Independence', before many recent events and changes had taken place: 'We in Bahrain, with all our economic, social and military strength can never contemplate isolating ourselves from our community in the Gulf and the Arab world. In this age, no power can fully sustain itself. The need for strategic depth and vast hinterlands is a requirement which has to be met. The world has shrunk due to the increased range of modern weaponry and the spread of communication and transport. That made it necessary for us to join our brothers in the Gulf in a common strategy and observe the same commitments as the rest of the Arab countries in this regard.' A multitude of far-reaching changes may occur in the world, the Arab countries, the Gulf region. We have to be ready to deal with them and adjust ourselves to them. Some of that has already occurred.

I am confident that the strategic principles expressed in the above passage remain, for Bahrain's people and leadership, absolute and unchanging fundamentals. If societies and nations have to adapt to changes, this cannot be achieved without holding on to national and religious fundamentals which are the foundation and framework of every entity large or small.

The torrent of change may uproot societies which do not hold firmly to their fundamentals.

These are beliefs which we in Bahrain will never abandon.